How to Dress
Like a Tudor

How to Dress Like a Tudor

Judith Arnopp

PEN & SWORD
HISTORY

First published in Great Britain in 2023 by
Pen & Sword History
An imprint of Pen & Sword Books Limited
Yorkshire – Philadelphia

Copyright © Judith Arnopp 2023

ISBN 978 1 39901 535 6

A CIP catalogue record for this book is
available from the British Library

Typeset by Mac Style
Printed in the UK by CPI Group (UK) Ltd, Croydon, CR0 4YY.

MIX
Paper | Supporting
responsible forestry
FSC
www.fsc.org   FSC® C013604

Pen & Sword Books Limited incorporates the imprints of After
the Battle, Atlas, Archaeology, Aviation, Discovery, Family History,
Fiction, History, Maritime, Military, Military Classics, Politics,
Select, Transport, True Crime, Air World, Frontline Publishing, Leo
Cooper, Remember When, Seaforth Publishing, The Praetorian Press,
Wharncliffe Local History, Wharncliffe Transport, Wharncliffe True
Crime and White Owl.

For a complete list of Pen & Sword titles please contact

PEN & SWORD BOOKS LIMITED
47 Church Street, Barnsley, South Yorkshire, S70 2AS, England
E-mail: enquiries@pen-and-sword.co.uk
Website: www.pen-and-sword.co.uk
or
PEN AND SWORD BOOKS
1950 Lawrence Rd, Havertown, PA 19083, USA
E-mail: Uspen-and-sword@casematepublishers.com
Website: www.penandswordbooks.com

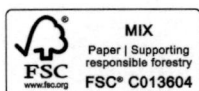

Contents

Acknowledgements

Writing this book during the Covid-19 pandemic proved trying. Historic attractions, museums, and libraries were closed, people were not permitted to meet, but somehow, I have managed to get the book written. I would not have been able to do so without the stoic support of several people. My partner, John, provided his invaluable opinions and proofreading skills, kept me supplied with ginger tea, and reminded me when it was time to eat. The support from my fabulous re-enactment group, The Fyne Companye of Cambria, kept me buoyant and when we finally were allowed to meet up, the talk of fabric and patterns and their first-hand knowledge of wearing Tudor clothes bolstered my sometimes flagging enthusiasm. Thank you to Lisa Lucas LRPS, Jane Mcilquham, Jeff Taylor, Simon Arnopp, and Lorna Mclean for generously allowing me to use their lovely photographs taken on our re-enactment days. I'd also like to thank my commissioning editor, Claire Hopkins, for guiding me through the process, and the Facebook group of fellow P&S authors, Wendy Dunn, Sharon Bennet Connolly, Paula Lofting, Brigette Webster, and Catherine Brooks, who listened to my worries, soothed me when I was pulling out my hair, and generally spurred me on. I will not forget that.

Preface

As an author of Tudor historical fiction, I have spent the greater part of my life reading, researching, studying, and writing about the Tudors. I mainly write about the women who shared their lives with Tudor monarchs, and I immerse myself daily in their world. Although I've studied all the Tudor kings in some depth, there is something about Henry and his wives that continues to fascinate each new generation. They are drawn by the intrigue, the duplicity, and the violence of the era – an era we like to reassure ourselves is quite different from our own.

As a teenager, I revelled in the fiction of historical authors like Rosemary Hawley Jarman, Jean Plaidy, and Maureen Peters. It was their novels that first lured me into history so when it was time for university, history and English literature seemed the natural choice. Two years after graduation, my first historical fiction novel was published. A few novels down the line found me with a stall at events which in turn led to me procuring my first Tudor gown.

When I attended my first Tudor event at Raglan Castle, I found myself in the company of King Richard III, Henry Tudor, knights and ladies, courtiers, craftspeople, and commoners from infants to mature adults. It was a complete revelation. For me, that day was the stuff of dreams.

On my return home, I immediately began to search for Tudor clothing of my own and to my delight managed to purchase a second-hand gown made by historical couturière, Gina Clark of Tudor Dreams. If I'm honest, it was a bit tight, but I managed to squeeze into it and over the next few years, I attended as many events as I could, taking my books along to sell to visitors. I really enjoyed the informality of sharing my knowledge about the castle, who lived in it and how, why it was built and by whom.

Since becoming a Tudor lady, I've been escorted to a joust by Henry VIII and even been beheaded for some crime of which I assure you I was innocent! But I expect they all say that. I loved dressing up so much that I wanted to belong to a group, but they are scarce in West Wales, and I am a poor traveller. Unable to find an existing local group, I got together with a couple of friends who share my passion and became one of three founder members of The Fyne Companye of Cambria – a medieval/Tudor re-enactment group. We now haunt some of the castles and manor houses of Wales – or we did until Covid-19 reared its ugly head. In the last couple of years, our hobby has been sadly impeded by recent restrictions but like every other re-enactor in the world, we can't wait to get back out there.

When the time came to replace my original gown, I discovered the price tag of a professionally tailored one was far above my meagre budget and despite lacking experience and armed with very modest sewing skills, I decided to attempt to make my own. The first gown I made was shockingly bad, but guessing that I'd probably fail, I'd had the foresight to make it from cheap second-hand curtains purchased from a charity shop. I was disappointed with the result and for a while I gave up the idea, despairing of ever making a wearable period garment. However, my mother taught me that you haven't failed until you stop trying, so I set to and began again, this time using better and considerably larger curtains.

My first few projects proved to be a steep learning curve, but I learned quickly and am still learning. I am by no means an expert sewer and have only school-level skills, but I quickly improved. I now know how to construct a stiffened bodice, how to pleat miles and miles of skirt into a tiny (well, it seems tiny) waistband. My methods are not always authentic, but I manage to produce French hoods, gabled hoods, coifs, and bags for fellow re-enactors and have also sewn a couple of medieval houppelande gowns, shifts and kirtles, and several more Tudor gowns. I also keep the men in our troupe kitted out, and recently completed a fine ensemble for the young Henry VIII and a set of clothes for the Duke of Norfolk, as

Figure 1: The Tudor monarchs – Henry VII, Henry VIII, Edward VI, Mary I, Elizabeth I (*Wikimedia Commons*)

well as a medieval costume for Richard Plantagenet, Duke of York. I am not and never will rank among the best sewers, but I hope to illustrate in this book that with research, patience, determination and sometimes a little bit of cheating, you too can dress like a Tudor.

Introduction

The Tudor period covers the years from 1485, when Henry Tudor won the crown from Richard III at Bosworth Field, to the death of Elizabeth I in 1603. It was an era that saw massive social, religious, and political change. Under the first Tudor monarch, Henry VII, English society and fashion remained pretty much as it had been in the medieval era. Although the king and his queen, Elizabeth of York, wore clothing to suit their status, made of the highest quality fabrics, their style lacked the splendour and ostentation of the reign that followed. Margaret Beaufort, Henry VII's intelligent and fiercely pious mother, spent an enormous sum on her nun-like clothing. Her black and white ensemble was made up of black damask, white silk, furred with ermine, and her nightgowns were lined with lambskin. She also had an unholy love for jewellery and spent heavily on 'gold rings set with rubies, gilded girdles and jewels of flowers with diamonds and rubies',[1] which goes to prove that costly clothing does not have to be magnificently sparkly.

It was the second Tudor king, Henry VIII, who made the biggest innovations in clothing. Henry was very much aware that the Tudor name was as yet unestablished as a royal house. When he came to the throne, the Tudors had only been in power for twenty-four years and were an unremarkable dynasty. The royalty of Europe sneered at the upstart kings sprung from a bastard line. Or at least, Henry perceived that to be the case and the new king set out to show the world exactly who they were dealing with. Throughout his life, Henry strove to be the best at everything, the best dancer, the best singer, the best poet, the best wrestler, the best horseman, the best man, the best king… ever.

If Henry understood anything, it was the importance of image, and this knowledge initiated the series of 'power portraits' that spoke silently yet eloquently of Tudor permanence and dominance, and if Henry was determined to make a lasting mark on the world, he certainly succeeded.

The iconic portrait of Henry, painted by Holbein the Younger when the king was in his prime, was taken after he had freed himself from Anne Boleyn and the Pope, and Jane Seymour had finally provided the son and heir he'd been craving.

We are used to this portrait now, and others like it, but imagine its impact in a world in which images were rare and people's lives were not dominated by photographs or colour as ours are today. Everything in this painting is designed to impress: we cannot take our eyes from the breadth of shoulder; the sumptuous quality of his clothes; his immovable stance; the potent codpiece; and the unflinching expression in his eye. The portrait exudes wealth, power, and uncompromising control. It is an unspoken declaration. 'I am the king; you *will* do as I say.' There is not the slightest hint of insecurity, yet Henry was very insecure.

We all know about Henry; his failed marriages, his quest for an heir, his break with Rome, his megalomania and ruthless rule, but what about the man behind the grandeur? Take a closer look at his face. What does it tell us about the inner man?

At first glance, he looks bullish, but on closer inspection you will see his eyes are blank, his expression closed. You might say he looks belligerent or mean but that may be a preconceived idea, because of what we already know of his reign. Personally, I think his inner feelings are obscured by our pre-knowledge but, if I try to wipe my mind and focus solely on his face, I see ennui, doubt, and sadness. As if he is hiding behind his own splendid construct.

All the Tudor monarchs have this same expression. The portraits are only concerned with an outward show of majesty, a declaration of authority. Edward VI was ten years old when he became king, a young skinny boy with a burgeoning ego that would soon match his father's.

He is carefully painted in a similar stance to Henry. He is well-padded, his vast coat embellished with satin and fur, and sports a much smaller codpiece than his father's, which still promises future virility and heirs to continue the Tudor name. But again, it is the image of a king with an empty face. 'I may be just a boy,' he is saying, 'but do not underestimate me; I am my father's son.'

Unlike her father and brother, Mary is seated in her portrait but is no less authoritative. Her erect posture and uncompromising stare are enough to turn living flesh into stone but there is little to be read there; we cannot see beyond her steely gaze to the woman within. Yet we now know that Mary was consumed with doubt, the instability of her upbringing stamped heavily on her psyche.

Her attempts to reinstate the Catholic religion and wipe out the much newer Protestant religion resulted in the burnings and torture that earned her the posthumous name 'Bloody Mary'. But Mary had lived a sorry life; rejected by her father, disinherited from the succession, stripped of her title 'princess', separated from her mother, Catherine of Aragon, Mary channelled all her frustration and anger into her religion. Her devotion to God and the Catholic Church was matched only by her passion for her husband, the reluctant Philip of Spain, and her wish for a son to follow her.

Her health was never good; there is some evidence that her menstrual cycle was erratic, and she suffered both physically and mentally from an early age. In later years, her failure to conceive, her phantom pregnancies, and failing marriage compounded her misery until she died a painful death in 1558, leaving no heir. Mary, who had gone to extreme lengths to rid England of the new religion, was now forced to pass the realm into the hands of a Protestant queen, her younger sister, Elizabeth, the daughter of Anne Boleyn.

Elizabeth was the greatest Tudor of them all and the one who exploited royal portraiture to the full. The queen was very aware of the power of image and iconography. Encouraged by her adviser, John Dee, her portraits became more and more extreme. Even during the early part of her reign, in every image, she is majestic and fabulously dressed, her tiny frame all but obliterated by satin, velvet, lace, and jewels. In looks, Elizabeth resembled her great-grandmother, Margaret Beaufort, and her grandfather, Henry VII, but by nature she was very much like her father.

If her grandfather and father had coveted England and parts of Europe, Elizabeth's ambitious eye went even farther, to the New World. In the Armada painting, her hand rests on a globe and, just in case the viewer should forget who wears it, the crown of England is just above. If you look closely, her famously long white fingers are covering the Americas and behind her are commemorative paintings of the Spanish fleet being driven onto a rocky shore by a storm that became known as the 'Protestant Wind', suggesting God's approval of England's victory over Catholic Spain. Elizabeth is proclaiming herself the saviour of her people;

the mother of her expanding empire: a victorious Virgin Queen, blessed by God.

These are the things the Tudors wanted the world to see and believe. Their private 'selves', their inner thoughts and feelings were none of our concern and so they turned their faces into masks, presenting a blank page devoid of personality yet replete with majesty. The strategy worked. No one ever links the name Tudor with the words 'weak' or 'powerless' and they achieved this reputation simply with the use of suitable clothing and exceptionally good artists.

The prize for the biggest innovation must go to Henry VIII. He initiated huge changes to England, in particular his break from the church in Rome. These changes resonated throughout Tudor society and can be detected by studying the homes they lived in, the churches they prayed in, and the clothes they wore.

During Henry's quest for a divorce from Catherine of Aragon and his desperation to make Anne Boleyn his wife, the king dispensed with the Pope and made himself Supreme Head of the Church in England. It wasn't just a case of ridding himself of papal rule and redirecting wealth that was paid to Rome into his own coffers. He dissolved the English monasteries and reduced ecclesiastical power within the realm itself. As usual, the people who this impacted the most were the poor, who relied on the great abbeys for employment and healthcare, and the effect it had on them should not be underestimated. A large part of the religious community was made homeless, without recourse to income. The roads of England became home to dispossessed monks and nuns and those years saw a huge increase in reports of vagrancy and poverty. At the other end of the spectrum, King Henry became more powerful and a good deal richer – and so did Cromwell, and the king's friends who benefitted from gifts or leases of former church land and properties. Henry now answered to no one other than God, and his sense of total supremacy can be seen, reflected in his changing image, traceable through contemporary royal portraiture.

The early images of Henry show a young man medieval in his dress, a man whose demeanour suggested he had the potential to become a learned and reasoned monarch. It was only after his break from Rome that his painted image altered into one of superhuman proportions. As his reign progressed, his eye became colder, his gaze more direct, and his clothes became increasingly magnificent. Portraits of his queens illustrate that they dressed to complement the king but never outshine him, and to a degree, as his courtiers aped his style, this new look trickled down the social scale.

Just as modern society trends in fashion are set by royal icons like the late Diana, Princess of Wales, or her daughter-in-law, Kate Middleton, so too did the higher strata of Henrician society copy their betters. Ordinary folk adopted the style to a lesser extent, hampered as they were by poverty and *sumptuary laws* that imposed restrictions on the way they dressed.

Sumptuary laws are described by *Black's Law Dictionary* as 'Laws made for the purpose of restraining luxury or extravagance, particularly against inordinate expenditures for apparel, food, furniture, etc.'

In England, such laws had been in place since the reign of Edward III in the fourteenth century, but Henry lost no time in extending them. At his first parliament in 1509, an Act Against Wearing Costly Apparel was passed, which laid down a firm dress code. It was decreed that only the royal family were allowed to wear purple silk or gold, yet portraits usually depict him in red, gold, and black. Dukes and marquises could use cloth of gold only when it was woven into coats or doublets. Fur was also prohibited, with only those above the rank of earl permitted to wear sable and jenet.

Certain servants of the royal chambers were allowed imported furs, as were landowners with an income of eleven pounds a year and above. Anyone below the rank of knight of the garter was prohibited from wearing 'velvet of crimson or blue'. Velvet, satin, and damask were also restricted to those below the rank of knight. Serving men were allowed less than three yards of fabric in a long gown, and two and half yards in a shorter one. These laws continued until Elizabeth's reign when the act was embellished still further to encompass the new, rather startling fashions of her era, adding rules on ruffs, hose, and the length of one's sword. Of course, rules were (and are) made to be broken and were difficult to enforce.

Clothes were often handed down to younger family members or servants. Garments were repurposed and often included in a will; it is highly likely that everyone, both higher and lower orders, broke this law to some degree. Imagine how tempting it would be for a lowly person to come into the possession of a small scrap of silk or velvet and use it to stealthily line a collar or pocket.

Among all classes of the period, an outfit was multi-layered. This was not only to provide extra warmth in the days before the invention of central heating, when the climate was several degrees cooler than now, but for the purposes of hygiene. The base layer was almost always made of linen; for the upper echelon, their fine linen (or sometimes silk) was usually embroidered or trimmed with lace. These underclothes needed to be tough enough to withstand regular scrubbing and the lower orders favoured a coarser fabric with little or no embellishment.

In both cases, linen absorbed sweat and provided a barrier between the skin and the delicate, and therefore more difficult to launder, outer layers. Linen was easy to wash and dry and relatively cheap to replace. Outer clothing was costly and even the upper classes would wish to extend its wearable life for as long as possible. Linen was changed frequently, outer clothing was sponged, or brushed and aired. To the modern mind, this sounds terribly unhygienic and our failure to accept that daily laundering was not necessary initiated the idea that the Tudor era must have been a very smelly place in which to live.

As a schoolgirl, I was taught that Tudors never bathed and if we met someone from that era, we'd find them repellent. While filming for *The Tudor Monastery Farm*, historian Ruth Goodman spent three months living and working and washing as a Tudor. She talks about the experience in her excellent and often amusing book *How to Be a Tudor*:

I wore all the correct period layers and head coverings. I was working on a farm, so this entailed a much heavier coarse linen smock, woollen hose and far fewer changes of underwear. Although I was working mostly outdoors, often engaged in heavy labour and also lurking around an open fire, I found that just changing my linen smock once a week proved acceptable both to me and to my colleagues – including those behind the camera, who had more conventional modern sensibilities. The woollen hose I changed just three times over the six months; the linen parts of the head-dress I changed weekly along with the smock. There was a slight smell, but it was mostly masked by the much stronger smell of woodsmoke.[3]

It seems that while a Tudor person may well have carried a different odour to a modern person, it was not necessarily an unpleasant one.

Figure 2: Medieval bath time. (*Unknown author, CC0, Wikimedia Commons*)

Unlike today, clothes were not a throwaway item. They were restyled or repurposed, reusing the fabric, the trims, or turning the seams. For an upper-class lady, the clothing layers were as follows.

A fine linen shift was often embellished with embroidery and lace. This garment was knee- or mid-calf-length with long sleeves and a wide square neck. Over this, a full-length kirtle was worn. This was laced at either the front, side, or back. Garments intended for court or social occasions sometimes had a short train, for less showy events the hem was floor level. Depending on status, kirtles could be made of silk, wool, or linen and were lined and sometimes padded.

After the kirtle, a gown was worn. Depending on the status of the wearer, it would be made of wool, silk, or velvet, usually with wide, hanging sleeves and laced at the front with a placket to cover the lacing.

The placket was pinned into place. Lastly, foresleeves were added, often slashed with silk, embroidered, and embellished with jewels. Many pieces of a lady's dress were interchangeable; sleeves and kirtles were made in different fabrics to be worn with various gowns for a completely fresh look. Usually, the sleeves and kirtle were in matching fabric; perhaps two pairs of similar sleeves were made, the larger, fancier ones for special occasions.

For chilly days, or perhaps modesty, a partlet helped stave off the cold; this covered the shoulders and chest and is depicted in many portraits. Some are made from velvet, some from a sheer fabric and sometimes it is so sheer you can barely see it. Later in the period, the partlet developed a high standing collar to complement the higher-neck shifts as they evolved into the Elizabethan ruff.

A lady's headwear would again be made up of layers; a linen coif not only protected her hood but provided somewhere to pin the outer hood and paste. A lady, particularly a married lady, would not be seen in public without a head covering, as it was deemed disrespectful to both God and the king.

A lower-class woman's garments would ape the shape of her betters and be made up of similar layers, but her clothes would be fashioned from cheaper coarser fabrics with little or no embellishment. There would

Figure 3: The author and her partner as Tudor tradesfolk. (*Photograph: J. Arnopp*)

be far less yardage in the skirt and hanging sleeves were replaced with removeable unadorned sleeves. A housewife or working woman would also wear an apron.

A merchant was as neatly presented as his wife, his clothes hardwearing and cut from the best cloth he could afford. The working and merchant classes dressed modestly yet decently to reflect their honest status, just as the king dressed flamboyantly to reflect his majesty, although in Henry's case, it was not perhaps such an honest statement.

Powerful. Brave. Confident. Those are the words Henry's portraits evoke, yet as mentioned previously, despite appearances, Henry VIII lacked confidence. As the second son of Henry VII, he had no expectation of the throne until the death of his elder brother, Arthur, the Prince of Wales. From the age of ten, Henry was suddenly subjected to an intense education on the requirements of kingship, the greatest lesson being a king's duty to beget an heir. In fact, it was advisable to have as many sons as one could manage because as the death of Arthur had proven, one or even two sons were simply not enough.

Shortly after his marriage to Catherine of Aragon, his brother's widow, Henry was overjoyed by the birth of a son. When that son died a few weeks later, his disappointment must have been immense. As years passed and Catherine continued to suffer failed pregnancies or give birth to children who died in the cradle, Henry became increasingly disillusioned.

Catherine was several years Henry's senior and there is little doubt he married her out of love, or knowing Henry, perhaps from the desire to possess all that his brother, Arthur, had once enjoyed. This first marriage was Henry's longest and, barring Catherine's failure to give him a son, for many

Figure 4: Catherine of Aragon wearing a gabled hood, portrait at Lambert Palace, unidentified painter. (*Public domain, Wikimedia Commons*)

years they were happy. She was an exemplary queen and, up until her death, an exemplary woman.

While Henry pursued war in France, Catherine stood as regent over England, during which time her army was victorious in the war with Scotland at the Battle of Flodden. She was loyal, strong, and noble but as the end of her fertile years approached and she had only managed to produce one daughter, the Princess Mary, Henry's concern at having no heir began to mutate into panic. He began to seek an escape from his marriage to Catherine of Aragon and decided take a younger, more fertile queen long before he set eyes on Anne Boleyn.

Once he became under the spell of Anne Boleyn, his desire to end his union with Catherine increased, and he had every expectation that the annulment would be quickly and simply achieved. He had not reckoned on Catherine's determination to protect her status as Queen of England and her daughter's position as Henry's legitimate heir. Henry's expectation wasn't as outrageous as it seems to us today. It was not unusual for women to retire to a nunnery, making way for their spouse to take a new fertile wife, but Catherine was having none of it, and she had the backing of the Pope.

The scandal of Henry's love life soon became the talk of Christendom. The heads of Europe were laughing at him, the matter became the butt of bar room jokes, and his need for a son escalated into an obsession. Shamed and emasculated by his lack of an heir, Henry VIII launched a massive Tudor publicity campaign, with himself assuming the role of the ultimate fashion icon.

In subsequent paintings, his projected image became one of control. Every inch of his pose suggests authority. His clothes, his stance, his direct stare, a statement of power and quite ironically, in hindsight, fertility.

If you examine his portraits closely, you will discover his expression is bland, his eyes are cold. Every fibre of his clothing is the finest that could be obtained, belying the nature of the man beneath – a man who was running scared, a man who had everything yet was denied the thing he desired the most – a son. Henry hid, or attempted to hide, his failings from the world by disappearing beneath the most splendid clothes he could obtain.

Like everyone else in Tudor England, closest to his skin, Henry wore a shift but while low-class men wore the roughest linen, Henry wore the

Figure 5: Henry VIII after Hans Holbein. (*Wikimedia Commons*)

finest silk. But rich or poor, even kings perspire, and his expensive shift served the same purpose as that of a ploughman; it absorbed sweat and odour and, in Henry's case, protected the costly outer layers.

Some sources say Henry's linen was changed four times a day, but I would imagine a peasant wore theirs for a good deal longer. Henry's shirt or shift was embellished at the collar and cuff with black or red work. In the past, it has been stated that blackwork embroidery was first introduced to England by Henry's first queen, Catherine of Aragon, but this has now been disproved. She is, however, thought to have personally embroidered Henry's shirts and continued to do so even after Anne Boleyn became his mistress, a situation which caused Anne much chagrin after she became his queen.

Henry's stockings were made of the finest silk. They reached his mid-thigh and were embellished below the knee with his most noble order of the garter, an order founded by Edward III in 1348. On his feet, he wore broad slashed shoes that resembled a bear's paw. They were often made of kid leather but sometimes they were of silk or velvet.

Next came the jerkin, or jacket as it later became known. As king, Henry's jerkin was made of cloth of gold, and fashionably slashed to show the silk finery beneath. It had a canvas inner to stiffen it and the lining was silk or fine linen. The front and sleeves were richly decorated with ouches (jewelled buttons), and bullion lace of gold or silver.

Nether hose or balloon hose served to cover the area between thigh and waist. They were secured to the jerkin with silk ties, tipped with gold aglets, threaded through loops or holes sewn into the waistbands. These fastenings were knowns as points and were also used to fasten women's kirtles and sleeves.

Over this came the kirtle (sometimes referred to as coat or jerkin). This was a knee-length, skirted, sleeveless gown, made of cloth of gold and embellished with bullion lace. The front was cut away with a large scoop at the chest to reveal the fancy jerkin beneath, and below the waist the skirt was worn open to show off the impressive codpiece.

Henry's codpiece is probably the most talked about item of Tudor dress. The codpiece originated during the medieval era as a small pouch to cover the genitalia in a way that conveniently facilitated urination but, like the Scottish sporran, it evolved into a convenient purse to house coin or small valuables. Like many other things under Henry VIII, the codpiece expanded to massive proportions, and rather ironically, came to be symbolic of male virility. The codpiece was as lavishly embellished as the rest of the outfit. It is interesting to note how the cut of Henry's kirtle, his stance, the line of his pendant, all draw the eye downward to the codpiece – a statement of unassailable regal fecundity.

A silk sash was tied about the waist both to hold the gown securely in place and to suspend a short dress sword or purse.

Next came a gown, made of velvet or fur. It was a heavy garment with a thick canvas inner and linen, silk, or sometimes a full fur lining. This garment had either short or detachable sleeves, and as if he were lacking in width, the upper part of the puff sleeve was boned to provide extra bulk to the outline.

The king's most famous style of hat is made of black velvet, embellished with pearls and a fancy ostrich feather. It is familiar to us from his

Figure 6: Catherine, Duchess of Suffolk wearing a gabled hood by Hans Holbein the Younger. (*Wikimedia Commons*)

portraits, but there is a fascinating hat in the Royal Collection known as the Bristowe hat that purports to have belonged to Henry.

It has been in the possession of the Bristowe family whose ancestor, Nicholas, was clerk of the Wardrobe and Beds from the 1530s to 1544. After that, he was appointed Clerk of the Jewels to Henry VIII, Edward VI, and Queens Mary and Elizabeth. The Bristowe family hold to a tradition that the hat was caught by Nicholas when Henry tossed it in the air at the surrender of Boulogne in 1544. Unfortunately, this story cannot be verified but it remains a great example of a high-status Tudor hat. It is faded now but was clearly once very smart, made of silk tufting, sporting a green feather, a silver button, and holes where jewels would have once been attached.

With his hat on his head, his chain of office in place, Henry was ready for his day.

As discussed earlier, just as we ape current fashions from the Parisian catwalk, so did the nobility ape the fashion set by Henry, hampered, of course, by the restrictions of sumptuary law. Even had the law not existed, it would probably not have been wise for court gentlemen to rival the king's splendour too closely. Even in his prime, Henry was always jealous of his reputation as the most splendid king in Christendom.

The royal court had a strict hierarchy which obviously began with the king and queen at the top of the pyramid. Then their siblings, children, aunts, and uncles who were also of royal birth. After that came the noble men and women who served as gentlewomen to the queen or as royal chamberers. Only those of gentle birth, the daughters of earls or barons, qualified for this position.

When she became queen, Catherine of Aragon was assigned a household numbering 160 people, most of whom were women. She had eight ladies in waiting, who were countesses and duchesses from the highest families in the land. She also had thirty maids of honour, most of whom were married to members of the king's household.

Servants at the court, those who lived and worked closest to the king and queen, were always of high rank, the sons and daughters of dukes and earls. Lower down the scale came the offspring of the well-bred but not necessarily super-rich. The honour of being part of the royal household was often a double-edged sword. Appointments were sought after because they brought great prestige, but it was an excruciatingly expensive position to maintain.

A young woman entering service in the royal court as maid of honour was required to have acceptable garments and the cost could be crippling. Careful use of fabric was key. It is fascinating to read through the accounts and discover the economic devices that were used. When the daughters of Lady Lisle were summoned to attend court, they had new gowns made but their kirtles were repurposed from the fabric of older garments.[4]

There was no shortage of snobbery, and no courtier would stoop to appear too often wearing the same outfit. In order to raise money to pay for new ones, the cast-offs were sold on, creating a lucrative trade in second-hand clothes. Clothing was hugely expensive. Eleri Lynn in her book, *Tudor Fashion*, says:

> Six months' wages for a labourer would buy barely a yard of cloth of gold, whilst a fine cloak would require more than three years' wages. Indeed Robert Dudley, the Earl of Leicester (1532–88) paid more for one suit than William Shakespeare paid for a house in Stratford-upon-Avon less than a decade later in 1597.[5]

This explains why so many lower-ranking members of the gentry were bankrupted by attending court. Clothing was indicative of status, of success, of social standing. The ladies of Elizabeth's court were supposed to complement but never outshine their queen. William Brenchley Rye's book, *England as Seen by Foreigners, in the Days of Elizabeth and James the First*, contains an extract from Paul Hentzner's travels in England circa 1598 which describes in exquisite detail the picture of the queen and her attendant ladies. It is clear from this passage that the ladies of court were not just required to serve the queen but also for embellishment.

> That day she was dressed in white silk, bordered with pearls of the size of beans, and over it a mantle of black silk shot with silver threads; her train was very long, the end of it borne by a marchioness; instead of a chain, she had an oblong collar of gold and jewels. As she went along in all this state and magnificence, she spoke very graciously, first to one, then to another (whether foreign ministers, or those who attend for different reasons), in English, French,

Figure 7: Elizabeth I, *The Rainbow Portrait*. Formerly attributed to Marcus Gheeraerts the Younger. (*Wikimedia Commons*)

and Italian; for besides being well skilled in Greek, Latin, and the languages I have mentioned, she is mistress of Spanish, Scotch, and Dutch (Belgicum). Whoever speaks to her, it is kneeling; now and then she raises some with her hand. While we were there, William Slawata, Bohemian baron, had letters to present to her; and she, after pulling off her glove, gave him her right hand to kiss, sparkling with rings and jewels – a mark of particular favour. Wherever she turned her face as she was going along, everybody fell down on their knees. The ladies of the court followed next to her, very handsome and well shaped, and for the most part dressed in white.

For all the importance placed upon clothing, apart from fragments of embroidery, a few coifs and Henry's (alleged) Bristowe hat and gilt-embroidered gloves, there are very few items of Tudor dress surviving. But there are a few items that take one's breath away.

In 2015, at a small church at Bacton in Herefordshire, an altar cloth that had been in the church's possession for centuries was identified as part of a gown that had once been worn by Queen Elizabeth I.

The remnant is made of cream-coloured silk and cloth of silver. It is beautifully embroidered with flowers and foliage in silk, and silver and gold thread.

The garment has been dated to around the 1590s and the pattern is remarkably similar to the kirtle Elizabeth is wearing in the famous *Rainbow Portrait*, which resides at Hatfield House. The altar cloth was first identified by Ruth Elizabeth Richardson, who was researching for a book about Blanche Parry, a close companion and servant to Elizabeth throughout her life. Parry's connection with both Bacton and the queen could not be ignored.

Her suspicions were confirmed by the curator at the Historic Royal Palaces, Eleri Lynn, who on recognising the quality of materials and the level of embroidery skill instinctively knew the fragment to be the remains of something special. It is known that Elizabeth bestowed many favours on Parry, and experts now believe it may have been sent to Bacton by the queen in recognition of the woman who had been at her side for so long: a last gift to a devoted and long-serving courtier.

Even before its provenance was known, the cloth was considered a sacred possession by the church and they'd had the altar cloth mounted and framed in oak and hung above the congregation, close to Blanche Parry's monument. Thankfully, they chose to hang it on the north-facing wall, safe from the damaging rays of the sun. It had hung there for almost 100 years before its rediscovery. At the time of writing, the Bacton Altar Cloth is on display at Hampton Court Palace together with the *Rainbow Portrait*, on loan from Hatfield House, so the two can be viewed together.

When I am out and about in my Tudor clothing, I am often asked how the Tudors managed to conduct daily tasks in such restricting garments. Of course, the highest-ranking Tudors didn't have to worry about daily tasks, they had servants to do their every bidding. Also, the court clothes I wear for events do not represent everyday dress. Henry's garments I described previously were state clothes for public or court appearances. At his leisure, in his privy quarters, he would have worn something more comfortable, perhaps an ankle-length loose gown, and out hunting, or on the tennis court, his clothes would necessarily have been lighter and more serviceable. Those lower down the social spectrum would have done the same. Even when I was a child growing up in the 1960s, everyone had their Sunday Best for church or visiting or walking in public. For day-to-day life, we wore older, more comfortable clothing. In the Tudor period, it was much the same. Lower-class women would have worked and played in plainer, older gowns we often hear referred to as 'workaday' clothes, keeping their best garments for high days and holidays.

There were two main styles of fashionable Tudor gown – the French Tudor gown is the style we are most familiar, with the square neckline, wide skirts, and huge hanging sleeves. Later in the period, what has become known as the English gown was introduced. This sported a higher neck, narrower skirts, and close-fitting sleeves.

Dressing like a Tudor remains an expensive enterprise today. Most re-enactors do their best to emulate Tudor dress as accurately as they can, but it isn't possible to be 100 per cent precise. For one thing, some of the fabrics mentioned in the records are no longer available and, for humanitarian reasons, the use of fur and other animal products has in most cases thankfully been replaced with faux fabrics. There are different degrees of authenticity. Re-enactors who can most closely represent the originals are an educational historical tool. By sewing, wearing, and washing and mending these garments, we understand more about how the Tudors lived and worked.

As I mentioned earlier, it wasn't until I spent my first weekend in a tight-fitting Tudor gown that I really empathised with the women I write about in my novels. As an author, working mostly from home, I spend most of my time in lose comfortable clothing, so a weekend in high-status Tudor clothes is a bit of a trial. The simplest task becomes difficult. If you forget to put your shoes on before you are laced into your top gown, there is no way you can bend down to fasten them without assistance. Long, wide sleeves hamper the tying of knots, the threading of needles, even holding a pen becomes difficult. I find them a burden but, of course, high-status women weren't expected to do these things themselves – that was the job of servants, and servants are something I lack.

The skirts are wide and heavy, running, even walking briskly is hazardous, and they snag on everything – rather like the cord of the vacuum cleaner, if there is something for it to get hooked on, it will find it.

Our weather is much warmer than it was in the sixteenth century. For the re-enactor, the clothes seem hot and heavy, and it should be remembered that silk is easily ruined. I usually starve all day in order to preserve my clothes from stains; a spot of sauce or a splash of coffee would require specialist cleaning. A bowl of soup in the lap would probably result in the need for a new gown.

Re-enactment should be fun, both for the re-enactor and the onlooker, but as with most things these days, there is no shortage of elitism – even mild bullying in some cases. It would be a lovely world if we could all afford the prohibitive costs of accurate garb but personally, I feel quarter should be given for those starting out, or with a tighter budget. As long as a re-enactor researches their role and presents an outwardly convincing historical figure that pleases the public, then I don't think it matters that the invisible parts of their kit aren't quite correct. I'd lay good money that those gold chains of office I see around the necks of royal re-enactors are only pewter sprayed with gold paint.

I don't claim authenticity. The clothing I make for our group is 'historically inspired'. Even though I study them, I haven't yet attempted to closely replicate a historical portrait. I don't pay as much attention to the inners, linings, or underpinnings that will never be seen. I tend to machine sew the long seams that are hidden from view, but the visible finishing is sewn by hand. Our aim is to engage with the public at the castles we visit and add to the visitor experience and stimulate an interest for a subject about which we are passionate. We are as close as needs be for our purposes.

It is important to avoid obviously synthetic fabric or wildly inaccurate fantasy costumes at a historic event, but I think it is possible to get a good look without using prohibitively expensive fabrics. The key thing, in my opinion, is to avoid anything too shiny because it usually is, and looks, cheap and fake. It is easier to appear authentic in lower-class costumes where 100 per cent wool can be substituted for wool/polyester blend, and linen for a linen/cotton blend. In many cases, old curtains, woollen blankets, and sheets that can be picked up at a charity shop for a few pounds or discovered at the back of granny's airing cupboard can work equally as well as fabric purchased at £80 a yard.

Even those who lack the resources for the best costume love history just as much as those who can afford to embrace authenticity, and presumably we all want to promote and share our love of the subject. This book is intended to highlight the requirements of Tudor dress and illustrate how the look can be achieved on a lower budget. I will mainly be referring to court clothes, but the same pattern and style can be used to create lower-class clothing from wool or linen (or similar replacement). Just leave off the fancy embellishments.

Fabric of the Tudor era

During the Middle Ages, the wool trade provided more than half England's wealth. So central was it to the country's economy that King Edward III ordered his Lord Chancellor to sit on a wool bale during council. This 'Woolsack' was symbolic of the importance of the wool trade to the economy of England. Even today, the Lord Speaker in the House of Lords sits on a red wool-stuffed cushion. In 1938, it was refilled with wool from the wool-producing countries of the Commonwealth.

Until the Tudor era, English trade was limited, exporting wool and cloth to the Low Countries – an area we now think of as the Netherlands, Luxembourg, and Belgium. Bruges was the main trading place but after it was abandoned by the Medici family, trade moved to Antwerp, just across the North Sea.

In England, the majority of sheep flocks were owned by monasteries and manorial lords, the trade and the wool production industry adding substantially to their already immense wealth. Some landowners built fulling mills and tenter yards on their property, where the raw product was turned into cloth. With English wool in such high demand, wool and cloth merchants became rich, owning as many as 30,000 sheep. They grew richer still when tax concessions were granted in return for providing monetary loans to the king.

Under the Plantagenets, Edward IV owned clothing made from imported damask silk and velvet, but he possessed a greater quantity of fine woollen garments. Whether this was to support the wool trade or because fine fabrics were difficult to acquire is open to debate. But as Eleri Lyn points out:

> the 1547 inventory of Henry VIII's goods recorded over 1,000 metres of cloth of tissue, while just a hundred years earlier, in 1443, less than 2 metres of this luxurious textile were purchased for use by Henry VI.[6]

By the time of Henry VIII, the demand for rich textiles was vast and required not just for clothing but also for wall tapestries, tents, cushions, and bed hangings. The best fabrics were costly, and only accessible by the super-rich. In 1509, Henry VIII purchased eighteen yards of cloth of gold, paying the equivalent of ten years' wages for a skilled tradesman. This, more than anything else, illustrates the economic gap between rich and poor.

Relative to income, fabric was hugely expensive and, despite the sumptuary laws restricting the richest materials from the lower strata of society, everyone strove to acquire the best fabric they could. Considering the length of time sumptuary laws were in place, and how often they were revised, there were few prosecutions, probably because the crime was too difficult to police and I suspect that in most cases, the law was ineffectual.

There were of course, only natural fibres available – wool, silk, and linen being the obvious ones, but those headings covered a multiple of different applications. Linen was used to produce buckram, a coarse canvas-type fabric used as stiffener and interlining. It was also used for canvas for rougher working clothes. At the other end of the scale, linen holland was a better type of cloth, the fine weave used for ruffs, aprons, and coifs or shirts. Cambric, also made from linen, was a high-quality fabric used by the higher echelon, and lawn was used by the elite for ruffs collars and cuffs.

Wool was also used to produce many different types of cloth: flannel, broadcloth, russet, and worsted, to name a few. The finer fabrics were used for petticoats and hose, while gowns and coats were made from broadcloth. The historical record is replete with fabrics few of us have even heard of today: for example, grogram and buffin, which *The Tudor Tailor* describes as a 'ribbed worsted, sometimes mixed with silk'.

Silk was strictly for the elite and came under headings like silk, velvet, satin, taffeta, sarcenet, grosgrain, and damask. These fabrics were expensive then, and they are expensive now. Unfortunately for the re-enactor, the Indian and Chinese silks readily available on the market today are not, strictly speaking, authentic, although occasionally a modern plain silk will serve the purpose for lining or sleeves.

There were also mixed fabrics available to Tudors. A linen and wool mix, known as linsey-wolsey, was used for gowns, coats, and petticoats among the lower classes, and fustian, a versatile material, was used for the upper-class gowns, kirtles, doublets, and sleeves. Chamlet was a lightweight silk, for the use of gowns, but the law stated it was suitable only for those with a minimum income of £40 a year. And cloth of gold, which was obviously only for the seriously classy, was exclusively for those within the court circle. Cloth of silver was also available, and something called tinsel, not the sharp sparkly stuff of a modern-day Christmas tree but a cheaper fabric, intended for the upper echelon.

Today, of course, some of these fabrics are not obtainable at all. In almost all cases, we can only compromise and use what is readily available... or affordable.

For the monarchy, the Tudor era was one of display and the pinnacle and best-known example of Tudor extravagance took place in 1520, when Henry VIII and King Francis I of France 'met' at what became known as the Field of the Cloth of Gold.

The meeting was held in Calais, which was then a province of England. The rivalry between the two kings came to a head when, together with an entourage of 6,000 each, they met face to face for the first time to seal an Anglo-French treaty. The kings, their chief courtiers and ministers were dressed in cloth of gold, but it wasn't just the clothes that were made of this. The British Library houses drawings thought to be the original designs for the 'tents'.

The English royal tent was no mean structure but was built from wood and canvas, decorated to resemble a palace, with stained glass and roundels as seen at Hampton Court Palace. Some reports even mention a wine fountain. The interior and exterior décor was made of the finest textiles. The tents were huge structures, divided internally by rich textile walls forming rooms and galleries, apartments, and chapels. The French erected a 120-foot-long pavilion clad entirely in gold, but King Henry never got to see that because it had to be dismantled due to the gales that blew up just prior to his arrival.

For eighteen days, the English and French kings showed off, like two roosters before a cock fight, each vying with the other to prove their superiority. There were feasts, dancing, sporting events and, on the surface, all was very merry. Underneath, however, things were strained. Francis was Henry's rival in both power and looks, and probably while in his cups, he challenged Francis to a wrestling match in which he was humiliatingly beaten. But he put on a brave face, went on to best the French king at archery, and they parted, seemingly as friends, on 24 June. The good feeling was not to last, however, and just one month later, in July, Henry broke his agreement with Francis, and agreed with Charles V, the Holy Roman Emperor, to make no further alliances with France for a period of two years. By the following year, England was drawn into a dispute between France and Rome and the short-lived peace in Europe was at an end.

The extravagant expenditure of the Field of the Cloth of Gold proved not merely a waste of money but has gone down in history as an empty display of monarchic arrogance. Today it stands as testament to the unimaginable wealth of kings and the importance of fine textiles across Europe. In the Tudor era, textiles were regarded more highly than any other art form in the period, including paintings.

But toward the end of Elizabeth I's reign, the persecution of Protestants in Antwerp resulted in many Dutch and Flemish immigrants, many of them skilled textile workers, escaping to England. Their input into the industry caused the English economy to swell but in the Low Countries it dwindled, and the imported textiles favoured in the royal court became more difficult to acquire. As a result, thanks to the influx of foreign weavers, the English weaving industry began to flourish.

The Tudor court evokes images of steel blades, armour, stone castles, dank prison cells, flames of heretic fires; one seldom associates the word Tudor with softness. Yet plush, luxurious fabrics were of vital importance.

The significance of textiles at the Tudor court cannot be overstated. Henry VIII surrounded himself with hangings, tapestries, carpets, as well as his clothes. It was everywhere. The fabrics were the richest, thickest,

Tho: Moor L'Chancelour.

Figure 8: Sir Thomas More by Hans Holbein the Younger. (*Wikimedia Commons*)

and costliest available, and it was not just the king. One of my favourite portraits when it comes to textiles is that of Thomas More, painted by Hans Holbein the Younger, now housed in the Frick Collection.

Sir Thomas More was a humanist scholar and statesman. He mentored the young prince Henry and rose to even greater power after Henry became king. His offices included Privy Councillor, Speaker of the House of Commons, and Lord Chancellor. He is famous for his resignation as Chancellor and his refusal to support Henry's divorce from Catherine of Aragon, and the king's title of Supreme Head of the Church in England. This led to his conviction for high treason and subsequent beheading. He was canonised in 1935. The portrait in question was painted in 1527, when More held the office of Chancellor of the Duchy of Lancaster.

More is often referred to as a 'saintly' man, a 'humanist', but it should not be forgotten that this humanitarian did not shy from torturing and sentencing heretics to be burned at the stake. But I digress... back to the painting.

There is little of the man himself in the portrait. His face is solemn and tense, perhaps understandably so when one considers the uncertainty of the times he lived in, the burdens he faced. His status is expressed by the array of sumptuous textiles that surround him. He is wearing official robes, his collar of esses bears the badge of Henry VIII – the man who would one day sign his death warrant – and his hands are resting on his lap, his arms clad in deep red velvet sleeves. His gown is made of black velvet – remember, a good dark black was a difficult shade to produce and therefore among the costliest. The gown is fur trimmed and probably fur lined. Thomas More was not the sort of man to allow himself to feel the cold. Behind him, the draped green curtain is as thick and opulent as his attire. These materials have been chosen deliberately to illustrate

Figure 9: Henry VIII, Henry VII, Elizabeth of York, and Jane Seymour by Hans Holbein the Younger. (*Wikimedia Commons*)

the sitter's wealth, his power, and the luxury he was able to afford. When viewing the painting, the viewer wants to reach out and evaluate the quality of the fabric, to run their fingers through the softness of his velvet sleeves.

The Tudor court was not a static geographical location. The court was mobile – wherever the king was, there was the 'court'. The relocation of court consisted of a huge entourage which moved from palace to palace, county to county, although the king seldom travelled north. Henry's only recorded progress north was in his latter years, when newly wed to Katherine Howard.

When the king travelled, his court came with him. It was a huge undertaking. Before the royal party departed, the royal officers were sent ahead to ensure accommodation and suitable arrangements were in place. This also included lodgings at nearby inns and private houses for the lowlier members of the court. The royal couple did not take just a few of their clothes but also their hangings, plate, and furniture, most importantly the royal bed.

Figure 10: The family of Sir Thomas More, sketch by Hans Holbein the Younger. (*Wikimedia Commons*)

In addition to their belongings, the Privy Council also went along, as did the king's household and their servants, the king's brewer, his musicians, his jesters, his physicians. And if the queen was with him, then her household went along too. Hosting a visit from the monarch, although a huge honour, was often ruinous. In 1602, Queen Elizabeth stayed for just three days with Sir Thomas Egerton at Harefield and the honour of the visit almost broke him. He was obliged to pay out for twenty-four lobsters, 624 chickens, 48,000 bricks, and new ovens to cook enough food for so many guests. It cost him £2,013 18s. 4d, which is around £10 million in today's money.[7] I'd imagine Egerton was the only man in England thanking God that Elizabeth wasn't married, or then he'd have had the consort's household to deal with also.

Chapter One

Underpinnings – What Lies Beneath

Before I discuss the clothes themselves, we should consider the lives of the women who wore them. The Tudor era was vastly different to today, so different that we cannot come close to imagining the reality of being a Tudor woman. The rules, expectations and restrictions placed on women began early. Elizabeth Norton in her book, *The Lives of Tudor Women*, tells us that this inequality began in the womb when it was believed girls obtained their souls at ninety days of gestation, but boys received theirs after only forty-four.

During their childhood, a girl's education was quite different to that of her brother, and mainly centred on how to attract a good husband and run an efficient household. She had to learn how to dance, how to dress, how to sew. It was considered dangerous for Latin or Greek to be taught to girls due to their natural proclivity to lewdness. There were, of course, exceptions to this, but highly educated women like Elizabeth Tudor and Margaret More were very much in the minority.

All women were subject to their father and, after marriage, to their husbands. They were prohibited from entering legal agreements or owning property. They were expected to run their husband's household and take charge of his estate or business during his absence. Catherine of Aragon and Katherine Parr both stood regent over England during the king's absence and both women did an exemplary job. This was a role they could never have undertaken without an education. It was considered their duty, as was handing back the reins of government immediately upon the king's return.

Women of all social classes were expected to marry; those who didn't either joined a nunnery or suffered the shame of dependency on their male siblings, making them both a financial burden and an embarrassment to the family. For those who did not marry, the sense of failure must have been immense.

Figure 11: Mary Clopton by Robert Peake the Elder. (*Wikimedia Commons*)

Once married, they were expected to produce children; those who failed to do so were always found to be at fault. It was never the failing of the husband. Lower-class women took charge of their children's upbringing but only as far as the father allowed. Upper-class women and royalty had some say in their children's education, but always subject to the husband's approval. Elizabeth of York spent more time than most queens with her children and after analysing hers and Henry's handwriting, David Starkey believes she may have taught her son (later to become Henry VIII) to write. This suggests a close relationship.

Henry was fortunate. While his elder brother Arthur was sent away to learn the intricacies of kingship, Henry remained at Eltham under the care of women, which some say explains how he became spoiled and demanding. Even after Arthur's sudden death and Henry's promotion to heir, he was kept at Richmond under the close scrutiny of his father and grandmother. Until his mother's death a short time later, he and the queen were unusually close. Most noble women had to accept their children being sent away to be educated. Upper-class boys and girls were sent away to be raised in noble households and most mothers had little input into their child's upbringing.

In many ways, poorer women had more freedom than their upper-class sisters. Married women were always under the rule of their spouse and the only way for a woman to gain some level of independence was to be widowed. A widow could own property, assume the running of her dead husband's business, employ apprentices, export, and import goods. Although refused absolute equality with her fellow businessmen, she could maintain her own livelihood for as long as she remained single.

Figure 12: The Fyne Companye of Cambria at Raglan Castle. (*Photograph: Lisa Lucas LRPS*)

If she remarried, of course, the business would pass to her new husband, which makes you wonder why so many women remarried.

To modern women, the idea of being told what one must do is difficult to accept. The generation of children I grew up with viewed the title of 'princess' as something to be envied. As an adult, I now understand that being a Tudor princess was anything but enviable. Elizabeth of York, the first Tudor queen, was married to Henry Tudor shortly after his victory over the Yorks at Bosworth Field. She had no say in the matter, but their marriage seems to have been a success. Of course, we tend to assume she did not welcome the match, but she was of Plantagenet blood after all, and they were an ambitious family. She was the Plantagenet heir and may have craved the position of queen, even if only through marriage.

Elizabeth's daughter, Margaret Tudor, was married off to the philandering king of Scotland who was her senior by many years. Mary Tudor (daughter of Henry VII) was married against her will to the elderly King of France – rumour has it that she danced him into his grave and once she was widowed, she lost no time in marrying the man of her choice – without the consent of King Henry. Mary Tudor (daughter of Henry VIII) was spurned, disowned, disinherited, bullied, and illegitimised before finally selecting Philip of Spain as her husband; a decision that proved disastrous. Elizabeth Tudor was also bastardised, neglected, bullied, abused, and ignored, but presumably she learned from the fates of her stepmothers that marriage was best avoided.

I have heard modern historians deny that women were pawns but I cannot agree. They certainly were expected to know their place but that does not mean that they were meek. Men sought to use women as pawns, but although some women resisted, most were powerless, even princesses. With the exception of Mary Tudor, who on the death of the elderly king of France took the opportunity to marry a man of her own choosing, refusal to comply could make the situation worse. The women I have mentioned here were exceptions. Most women bore the daily restrictions placed upon them and went about their lives without rebelling. That doesn't mean life was easy. They were tough and should be admired for their stoic endurance.

As well as the social and physical rules they were subjected to, even their clothing was restrictive. Before the Tudor era, female clothing draped the figure, it did not seek to alter the shape or restrict movement.

Medieval clothing was soft and fluid, working with the body rather than against it. The Tudors changed that. During the reign of Henry VIII, through to that of Elizabeth, the female form, for the upper classes at least, gradually became imprisoned and moulded, and forced to comply, just like the wearer.

Researching historic clothing is time consuming and frustrating. One difficulty being that almost all reference to it is via records detailing something else – a description of an event that briefly mentions the queen's gown, or an account of a masque that details the theatrical costumes. It is unfortunate that someone in Tudor England didn't sit down and write an illustrated book on clothing throughout the age. I've found the easiest and most pleasurable resource for study to be portraiture, but it should be borne in mind that even artists sometimes distort the truth.

When researching Tudor fashion, I rely heavily on portraiture, but paintings of the period, while detailing the sumptuous outer layers, reveal next to nothing of what was going on beneath. Our knowledge of Tudor underpinnings is largely gleaned from wills or merchant records which inform us not only what Tudors were wearing but who was wearing them and what items they deemed worthy of bequest. These records do not always describe the style of the item but the fact it was valued enough to bequeath to a loved one suggests it was of significance to the original owner.

The purpose of the inner, hidden layers in the Tudor era was not just hygiene but, particularly in the case of ladies, it also helped define the required body shape. As I mentioned in the introduction, everyone wore a *chemise*, often referred to as a *shift* or *smock*, next to their skin. It was a loose, simple garment made from linen or silk, and the higher your status, the finer and whiter your shift would be. Lower classes wore coarse unembellished *shifts*, but the higher echelons favoured a fine linen cambric fabric or silk which was embroidered and frilled, the neckline and sleeves often decorated with an early form of lace, known as drawn thread work.

Linen is easy to wash and dry. It also absorbs sweat and protects the finer upper layers from dirt and staining. Shifts were not full length but ended around the knee to mid-calf. In the early period, the neckline would have been square, to mirror the fashionable neckline of the top gown, but later the shifts developed a neat high frilled collar that would eventually evolve further into the Elizabethan ruff. It was essential in polite society to wear clean linen every day. Henry VIII reputedly changed his up to four times every day.

In previous eras, clothing for both males and females had been practical in nature – the clothes of the upper classes were layered, they draped the body in a sumptuous yet comfortable manner. It is during the Tudor

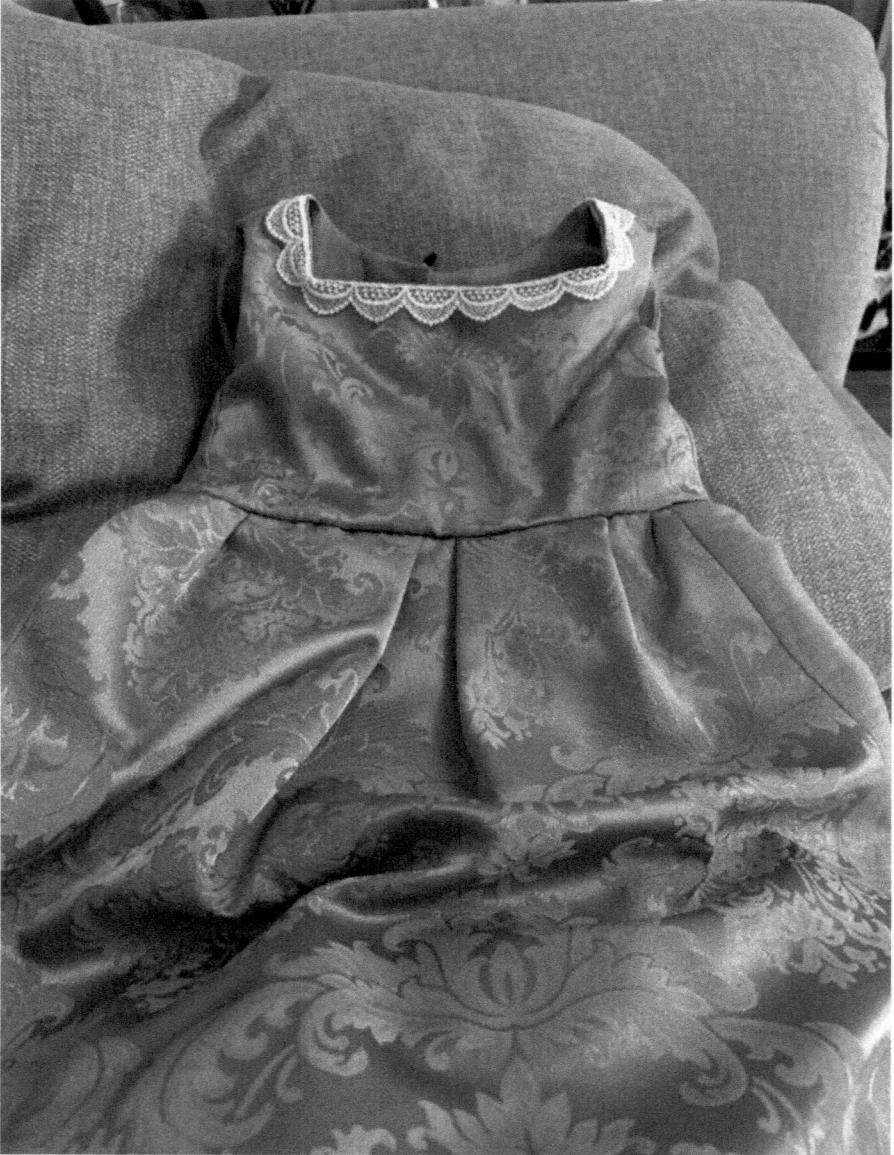

Figure 13: Child's kirtle. (*Photograph: Judith Arnopp*)

period that this begins to change. Although the iconic Tudor square neckline first appeared during the reign of Henry VII and the bodice became more rigid during the time of his son, as yet there were no corsets. The upper bodice of the top gown did the job of holding and masking the upper body. It was stiffened with paste buckram, padded to disguise the natural contours, yet one would imagine they were still relatively comfortable to wear.

At this time, the bodice was not completely stiff to hide the form beneath. In Holbein the Younger's sketch of Thomas More's family, the contours of his wife and daughter's upper torsos are clearly discernible beneath their clothes. During Elizabeth's reign, the fashion for stiff elongated bodices was introduced, which completely flattened the torso beneath.

The stiffened bodice served until the reign of Mary I when the first references appear to 'pairs of bodies' as a separate foundation garment. This late addition to the royal wardrobe may or may not have been to do with misinterpretation of language – at the time, the words 'bodice' and 'bodies' were interchangeable and could have obscured exactly when they were first introduced. Sarah A. Bendall, in her book, *Shaping Femininity: Foundation Garments, the Body and Women in Early Modern England*, suggests the late arrival of 'bodies' in England may be linked to Henry VIII's rather touchy relationship with Spain. He would not have welcomed innovative new Spanish fashion into his court, but Mary had quite different ideas and supported everything from her mother's homeland. After marrying King Philip II, she championed all things Spanish, despite her husband's neglect.

Indeed, rivalries amongst Renaissance princes, notably Charles V, King of Spain and Emperor of the Holy Roman Empire, King Francis I of France and King Henry VIII of England, encouraged the spread of Renaissance humanism, art and culture throughout Europe, and this competitiveness further opened the Tudor court to new fashion influences from places like Italy and Spain. The slow uptake of Spanish fashions by the Tudor court, as evidenced by the Spanish farthingale, may account for why references to bodies that were separate from gowns did not appear frequently in archival records until the reign of Mary I in the mid 1550s.[1]

At this stage, the 'bodies' were not boned but stiffened with buckram in the same way that kirtle bodices had been previously. It was under Queen Mary's sister, Elizabeth I, that the female outline altered drastically and harsher methods of controlling the figure were introduced. At this time, 'bodies' or bodices became outer wear, replacing the role of the kirtle.

The ideal Elizabethan image was about as far from natural as it is possible to be. These 'bodies' forced the torso into a cylindrical and rigid

Figure 14: Queen Elizabeth I, Crispin van de Passe, after Oliver. (*Wikimedia Commons*)

shape and carried the eye downward to a sharp point that ended just above the genitalia. The addition of a 'cartwheel' type structure beneath the skirt that formed a 'table' around the sides and back of the waist further altered the outline. Together with the huge ruffs and sleeves and the fashion for heavily made-up lead-white faces, this style has become the iconic Elizabethan image; a fashion led, of course, by the queen herself.

It has been suggested that this manipulation of form was to improve on the female shape, but I am more inclined to view it as an *erasure* of the natural feminine outline. As if this fashion wasn't uncomfortable enough, a busk was also introduced during this period. A busk was a long piece of wood, bone, or horn that was placed centre front between the body and the shift, to straighten the torso and remove any indication of breasts or belly beneath. Sometimes they were inserted into a stitched twin seam at the front of the bodies. I've never worn a busk, but I'd imagine it made bending down difficult. Luckily, Queen Elizabeth had servants to pick things up from the floor.

Initially the bodies were made with attached skirts, which became known as 'petticoat bodies'. It was not until later that they evolved into a separate garment. Toward the end of Elizabeth's reign, whale bone was used by the royal tailors and these garments were subsequently referred to as 'whalebone bodies' or 'French bodies'.

There are a few extant examples of 'bodies' from the late Elizabethan period, the most notable being those from the burial effigy of Elizabeth I. These bodies were probably constructed after Elizabeth's death by the queen's tailor, William Jones. They were placed upon an effigy of the queen that would be on display and accompany her casket to Westminster for burial. Clothing historian Janet Arnold thinks it unlikely the queen ever actually wore them but believes they were more likely to have been based on a pair Jones had previously made for the queen. The bodies inform us as to Elizabeth's size and reveal much about the construction techniques of the period. The bodies are tiny, fully boned with whalebone (baleen), and are front laced with no central busk. They are housed and on display at Westminster Abbey.

The word 'petticoat' derives from the French word for 'little coat' and in the early Tudor era, both sexes wore them, although they differed in style. They were often red, a hue which was believed to be beneficial to the health. The skirt was either mid-calf or floor-length, some with a bodice

Anna Bollein Queen.

Figure 15: Anne Boleyn sketch, Hans Holbein the Younger, (*Wikimedia Commons*)

attached, but some examples had a scooped front that fastened at the waist with laces. This not only reduced the quantity of fabric required but also decreased bulk over the bust. Interlined with wool or canvas, the garment provided extra warmth, and when worn with a Spanish farthingale helped to disguise the hoops beneath.

The Spanish farthingale is believed to have been introduced by Catherine of Aragon when she arrived in England to marry Prince Arthur. The ladies of the court were slow to adopt the fashion, but it did eventually become popular. Despite it being an undergarment, it was not exclusively made from linen or calico but often in bright colours and in a range of fine fabrics. The farthingale was stiffened with hoops which provided the typical bell-shaped Tudor outline we are familiar with. Today, most re-enactors' hoops are made from metal or plastic, available from most haberdashers, but during the period, rope, reed, cane, or even wood was used. Narrow channels are sewn horizontally into the skirt of the petticoat to keep the hoops in place and both Tudor and modern-day hoops are easily removable when the time comes to launder it.

Hose, a form of stockings, were worn by both sexes; they were either knitted or made from fabric. Women's hose tied beneath the knee with a garter, the top turned over rather like an old-fashioned football sock. The garters were made either from linen or wool and, since they were never seen, were only for warmth. The men's hose evolved during the period; originally, they were two separate garments that reached the upper thigh and were tied with points but later were joined at the back with a flap at the front that we know as the codpiece. I will discuss this item of clothing in more detail in the 'Men's Clothing' section.

I never dreamed the day would come when I would wear an item of underwear to make my bottom appear larger than it really is, but the bum roll does just that. The Tudor shape is impossible to achieve without one. The bum roll or 'roll', as it was referred to at the time, is made from calico or similar fabric and tightly stuffed with wadding. It ties around the waist over the farthingale to provide a becoming fall for the back pleats on the upper layers.

The first reference to a roll is in 1580 in the wardrobe account of Elizabeth I, but judging from earlier Tudor paintings, a similar effect was possibly achieved by small rolls of fabric being sewn into the back pleats of the gown. I've not yet tried this method.

In historical fiction, you often read rather garbled references to petticoats and corsets, and in my earlier books, I was probably guilty of it myself, but there were no corsets; stiffened bodices were the thing. Separate corsets, or bodies as they were known, came later in the period. One might expect a corset or a pair of 'bodies' to be the next layer in the French-style gown but during the Henrician era, the outline was created by the bodices of the kirtle and the top gown being stiffened with buckram and padding. I will discuss this further in the next chapter.

Surprisingly, one item of clothing which is absent from historical record of Tudor underwear is knickers or drawers. There has been much discussion as to how women of the era dealt with their monthly courses, blood loss following childbirth, or stress incontinence in later life. Until recently, it has been widely accepted that they wore nothing at all but during excavations at Lengberg Castle in East Tyrol, a pair of what look very much like knickers and several 'bras' were discovered. The discovery raised global interest, the tabloids taking delight in the skimpy nature of the finds.

During reconstruction of the castle in July 2008, a vault was discovered beneath the floorboards containing a collection of clothing that was dated to the fifteenth century. Although this is before the Tudor period, it is interesting to note that the idea of 'underclothes' may not, after all, have been overlooked. It may just be the case that examples did not survive and they are not mentioned in wills because… well, who'd want to receive someone's old drawers in a bequest?

Linen is pretty much indestructible and, among other items, there were several well-preserved linen garments that very much resembled modern bras and a pair of knickers. The tabloid newspapers became over-excited and dubbed it a medieval bikini, but can they really be what they seem?

The remnants of the knickers bear a resemblance to those worn by men in the fourteenth and fifteenth centuries when split hose (two single legs) were replaced with full hose, which had a back joining seam. There is nothing to indicate whether these items from Lengberg Castle were worn by a male or female, and it has been suggested that rather than 'knickers' as we know them for daily use, the garment was designed to be worn during menstruation or after childbirth. The items in question are well worn and have been repaired with linen patches. As a historian, I tend to prefer archaeological finds to be backed up with written evidence, but this discovery is difficult to dismiss.

Before now, it has been widely accepted that women did not wear drawers until the end of the eighteenth century. Most of the visual references I could find to women in pants are subversive in nature, lampoons of women in their spouse's hose, providing a social commentary on hen-pecked husbands and adultery. A woman in underpants was symbolic of the wife assuming her spouse's power because during the era, full hose (or trousers) were viewed wholly as a masculine article of clothing. A few instances predating the Tudor period, however, do point to evidence of female undergarments.

During a rape trial in Paris in 1337, two young apprentices were sexually assaulted and the account states that the attacker forced the girl into a cellar, threw her to the floor, and pulled down her 'brais'. Brais were an undergarment broadly resembling long drawers that are usually associated with men; there are a few other references that attach them to women, but they are all from the earlier period. It is unlikely that women of the late medieval or early Tudor period, accustomed to wearing them, would suddenly have abandoned the wearing of brais. Further to this, some form of feminine 'knicker' must have been worn during menstruation or after childbirth. But is that what has been discovered at Lengberg?

To my untrained eye, the so-called 'knickers' look very masculine. There is no delicacy of construction that is notable in other ladies' clothing from the period; they even seem to have room in the front to accommodate male genitalia. So, while this discovery is intriguing, I think we should not leap to conclusions. If this type of underwear was in widespread use, surely there would be reference to them in the record, or more examples discovered. There are a few mentions of Elizabeth I owning 'double linen hose' but that could refer to stockings, and Samuel Pepys refers to his wife's 'drawers', but these reports were both made considerably later than either our period of study or the carbon dating of the finds.

Regarding the so-called bras found at Lengberg, some reference can be found in early medieval documents to 'breast bags', but they are sketchy in detail. I can only form an opinion from the photographs that circled the internet at the time of discovery and if it weren't for the radiocarbon date of late fourteenth to mid-fifteenth century, I'd think they were far later.

Although undoubtedly designed to constrain and shape breasts, the Lengberg 'bras' were not the garment as we know it today. Two of the items seem to be part of a larger piece of clothing with bags (one for each breast), but since only fragments survive of each, it is difficult to be sure. We have only one complete 'bag' from each bra and there seems to have been extra fabric across the cleavage area, perhaps to provide a squared neckline, or perhaps for extra support. The garment seems to have ended just beneath the breasts.

The third garment is more recognisable as a bra, with two shoulder straps and surviving indications of a back strap. There are signs of decorative lace and braid.

The fourth resembles an old-fashioned long-line bra, with shoulder straps and lace. The cups are made from two pieces of linen, with a further piece of fabric that extends down the ribcage. There are also eyelet holes to suggest the garment was secured at the side with laces, rather like a kirtle. Perhaps it is the remnants of a kirtle.

During the Tudor period, it was more usual to have the bust flattened rather than accentuated but during the medieval period, there was a fashion for 'apple shaped breasts'. This style may have led to the invention of 'breast bags'. To back up these references, there are manuscripts from the mid-fifteenth century illustrating women with small round breasts, lifted and separated, so they look like small hard apples. How they achieved this look has long been in question. Fifteenth-century tailors had no elastic or Lycra, or anything remotely similar, but examination of the construction techniques used in the Lengberg discoveries suggest that what they lacked in modern materials, they made up for in skill.

To achieve the desired 'apple' shaped breasts, the cups (or breast bags) needed to be sewn by someone with knowledge of working with fabric on the bias. The cups are constructed from a finer linen than the rest of the garment, and each cup is made of two vertical halves, cut on the straight grain of the fabric. The two pieces are not precisely symmetrical, which would have assisted with support and encouraged both breasts to face forward.

To help keep the garment close-fitting, a front centre seam was inserted, and it is still possible to see fragments of lace in the space between the cups. This was not only decorative but would have added support and helped the cups lie flat against the skin.

If the garment had ended just below the breasts like a modern bra, it would have been very unlikely to stay in place. It would have rolled up from the bottom and provided little support, as well as being uncomfortable to wear. Close examination reveals tiny needle holes and a few strands of linen thread suggest that skirts had once been attached to the bottom of the 'bra'. This makes sense, for the weight of the skirts would have helped keep it from rolling up. Eyelets show that the garment was fastened by side lacing which not only provided a snug fit but also allowed for fluctuation in the wearer's weight, such as during pregnancy.

Since the archaeological finds, popular media has shouted, loudly and excitedly, about the discovery of medieval bra and knickers, some publications even going as far as to describe the garments as a bikini. However, the bras were undoubtedly part of a larger, skirted garment. I am not convinced that a society that covered the body so entirely with clothing would have conceived the idea of such skimpy undergarments. In my humble and inexpert opinion, I believe the discovery to be the fragment of a supportive shift, perhaps intended for larger ladies, worn close to the skin.

Being a generously proportioned lady myself, my own re-enactment solution is to wear a regular loose shift with a supportive kirtle, but during the course of the day, things do tend to… erm… slide. The idea of a medieval 'bra' has inspired many re-enactors to attempt a reconstruction, which is something I'd love to attempt myself in the future. For information on how to go about this, search 'supportive medieval kirtle' on YouTube and you will discover explanatory videos on the subject.

Chapter Two

Kirtles

The Tudor 'kirtle' evolved from garments worn in earlier eras and the word has evolved with it. During the medieval period, the word referred to the outermost layer of a lady's clothing, or what we would call a dress today. Over time, the loose-fitting belted garments of the medieval period gradually became closer fitting, eventually worn beneath a tabard or gown. By the early Tudor period, the kirtle had

Figure 16: Cecily Heron, by Hans Holbein the Younger. (*Wikimedia Commons*)

become a figure-hugging, laced garment with a full skirt that flared from the waist. Upper classes wore an additional, more extravagant gown over the top, not only for extra warmth but to flaunt their wealth and status.

By the reign of Henry VIII, the kirtle was a supportive garment worn over the smock and farthingale. The kirtle was full length, rather like a sleeveless dress. The bodice was usually stiffened with buckram (a reinforced canvas), to support the body and provide the required outline. The garment was laced either at the front, side, or back.

It is sometimes said that only those rich enough to employ maids opted for a back-lacing gown but there are plenty of painted images of lower-class women with back lacings – perhaps they had an obliging sister or daughter to help them dress. Front- and side-lacing kirtles allowed for a woman's changing shape during pregnancy and facilitated breastfeeding for the lower classes. Upper-class women generally employed a wet nurse to feed their babies, since breastfeeding delayed the return of the monthly courses, and it was important that the mother (especially queens) resume her fertility as quickly as possible.

The skirt of the kirtle at this time was usually padded or made from thick brocade to prevent the hoops of the farthingale from showing through the fabric. Prior to the reign of Henry VIII, the kirtle was quite a plain serviceable garment made of black worsted or something similar, but after his accession to the throne, the ladies and gentlewomen attendant on the queen began to wear fabric previously only worn by royals. Tawny, black, and russet satin and damask became increasingly fashionable and the overall look more splendid to do justice to the flamboyant king. As the era progressed, the fashions changed, and by the reign of Mary I, the kirtle ceased to be a one-piece garment. The bodice was dispensed with, leaving a half kirtle, a garment later referred to as 'petticoat'. To make things even more confusing, by the nineteenth century, the word 'kirtle' referred to a woman's short jacket but since that is outside our period, it won't concern us here.

Largely due to the manner in which this item of clothing evolved, there are varied and often conflicting references to them in the record. In some instances, the neckline of the kirtle itself was embellished with embroidery and jewels and was clearly intended to be seen, but sometimes it was a plainer garment, although still of the finest fabric, clearly not expected to be visible.

In the latter case, a 'forepart' was worn. This was an apron-like garment that tied about the waist and fastened to the bottom of the outer gown. It was made with the most luxurious fabric the wearer could afford and was always worn with matching fore sleeves. Both forepart and sleeves were usually embellished with pearls, and gold or silver embroidery. The forepart and sleeves could then be worn with different outer gowns to provide an alternative look.

The neckline of the full-length kirtle was just visible at the neck of the outer gown and adorned with jewelled ouches (brooches), pearls, and gold braid. Lower-class women would wear their much plainer kirtles with a jacket and apron, creating a neat, business-like appearance. Upper-class ladies had yet another heavy layer worn over the kirtle, which I will discuss later.

Before you begin to sew a kirtle, it is important to pay attention to the fit. It is advisable to make a toile – which is a sample or practice garment to try out the fit and make any necessary corrections without ruining your good fabric. This should be made from cheap non-stretch material like calico or something of equal weight. When making a kirtle or gown, it is only really necessary to do this with the bodice, where a good fit is essential, there is no need to waste fabric and time to make the whole garment.

Follow the instructions on the pattern until you have a well-fitting wearable bodice. Then you can either get someone to pin you into it or make rough lacing holes so you can fasten it in the same way you will the final piece. Always try it on *over* your shift and ensure the necklines of both garments complement each other. The shift edge should be just visible above the edge of the kirtle which, in turn, will be visible above the edge of the top gown when you come to make it. The fit of the shoulders and neckline is vital, as it will impact on comfort and the fit and look of all subsequent layers. It will probably require some trimming, pinning, and adjustment to achieve a good fit to your unique contours.

The Tudor Tailor has some authentic patterns but remember, unlike the less accurate patterns by Simplicity or Burda, Tudor Tailor do not include a seam allowance, so the fabric must be cut three-quarters of an inch larger all round. There are cheaper patterns than the Tudor Tailor's available, and although they are not historically accurate, it is possible to adapt them to ensure the final garment is more acceptable, but it requires a good deal of research.

Once you are satisfied with the fit, my advice is to make your first kirtle from cheap fabric. I often buy second-hand damask-style curtains at the charity shop – don't throw away the curtain lining, as it is useful for toiles. In my early days of sewing, I even managed to scrounge my sister's cotton velvet curtains from her front room to make a Tudor court outfit for my husband.

Chapter Three

Over Gowns

The over gown, or top gown as it is sometimes called, not only provided extra warmth but also enabled the wearer to advertise the fact that they could afford the luxury of an extra layer. In all classes, the gown was made of the best-quality fabric the wearer could afford. For the lower classes, this would have been wool, but the upper classes opted for silk or taffeta. Both sexes wore an over gown; the male version could be short, knee-length, or ankle-length. Clerics, lawyers, and academics wore plain dark-hued gowns as they went about their daily duties, but it was a cumbersome garment and most lower-class people would have worn just the kirtle layer during their working day.

In middling classes, those that could afford an extra layer while adhering to the sumptuary laws wore a gown of a similar style to the higher echelons but it was made from twill. This was a cheaper fabric dyed with what was known as 'poor black', a less dense dye than their betters could afford. The gown was lined with linen but the parts that might be seen, the cuffs for example, would be cut from the same fabric as the outside.

At court, the gown became an ostentatious display of the wearer's wealth and status. The width of the skirts, the length of one's train, illustrated that one could afford an infinite amount of fabric. The quality of cloth and the amount of embellishment further enhanced the statement of their social position. In the earlier period, over gowns or top gowns were relatively modest garments, but as Henry VIII's clothes grew ever more splendid, so did those of his courtiers. At her coronation in June 1533, Edward Hall described Anne Boleyn as she processed to Westminster:

> … she herself going under a rich canopy of cloth of gold, dressed in a kirtle of crimson velvet decorated with ermine, and a robe of purple velvet decorated with ermine over that, and a rich coronet with a cap of pearls and stones on her head; and the old duchess of Norfolk carrying her train in a robe of scarlet with a coronet of gold on her

cap, and Lord Burgh, the queen's Chamberlain, supporting the train in the middle.

After her followed ten ladies in robes of scarlet trimmed with ermine and round coronets of gold on their heads; and next after them all the queen's maids in gowns of scarlet edged with white Baltic fur.[1]

Nothing was too good for Anne Boleyn during this period. This coronation, as always, was the event of the era. Eager to show off his none-too-popular queen, Henry demanded a dazzling affair. Perhaps it was his way of persuading the public to see Anne as he did, but if this was

Figure 17: Lady wearing an English hood, costume study by Hans Holbein the Younger. (*Wikimedia Commons*)

the case, it didn't work. Despite her intelligence, her efforts for the poor, and for church reform, she was never popular with the commoners.

But, of course, even queens did not dress in splendour every day. When at leisure, Anne and her attendants would have worn loose gowns of fine but not quite so splendid fabrics.

By Elizabeth's reign, for the queen and her noble attendants, the decoration on the court gowns had exploded into a gaudy display of royal excess. Elizabeth's garments, or at least those she chose to wear in her portraits, were stiff, encrusted with diamonds and pearls and gold. It is highly probable that during her private hours, she would have opted for something more comfortable. What is very clear is that Elizabeth I loved clothes. At the time of her death, she owned 2,000 gowns, some of which were reused later in the next reign. By this time, Elizabeth's style was becoming outmoded but still of some use to Anne of Denmark, queen consort to King James VI and I. During her first court masque, *The Vision of the Twelve Goddesses*, Queen Anne requested the removal of Elizabeth's garments from the Tower of London for use in the performance. It is possible that other garments once belonging to Queen Elizabeth were repurposed in this way.

During the early Tudor period, lower-class women favoured a level hem, and they wore pattens on their feet to raise them and protect them from the mud and muck of the town streets. Merchant classes preferred a level hem too. However, in court circles, a short train became a feature on the French-style gown. This style of dress already had voluminous skirts to cover the farthingale petticoat and wide-skirted kirtle and the addition of a short train, and very wide outer sleeves, made it even more splendid as the period progressed.

The outer sleeves were often trimmed with velvet or fur, turned back at the cuff, to display the lavishly embellished and jewelled inner sleeves. There are some indications that for warmth, the bodices of some gowns were entirely lined with fur. A fur edging can be glimpsed on some of the portraits but whether this is a trim, or a full lining, is a difficult matter to establish. Of course, a full fur lining would only have been for the highest in the land. A queen or duchess could afford every comfort at a time when the temperature was a few degrees cooler than today, and thick stone castles were notoriously cold. A fur lining would have been cosy and if it were difficult to care for, well, that was a problem for the royal chamberer and the launderesses, not the queen.

Chapter Four

Women's Accessories

Headwear was of vital importance, especially for women who, once married, did not show their hair to anyone other than their husbands. Even in the privacy of their homes, the hair was covered by a coif. It was, in fact, considered bad manners to appear before God bare headed. From as early as the tenth century, both men and women wore coifs – a simple cap made of linen, or silk if your status and purse allowed. They were worn beneath hoods and caps, serving not only to keep the wearer warm but to keep the hair tidy and protect the lining fabric of expensive outer headwear from grease, in much the same way the linen shift protected the fine kirtle. Throughout the period, even as the fashion for hoods and hats evolved, a plain coif known as a 'biggin' that fastened with ties beneath the chin continued to be worn by babies, children, old men, lawyers, and doctors, usually beneath their hats.

There seem to have been several styles; from the simple biggin that fastened beneath the chin, to more complex headwear involving several layers and the inevitable pins. During the sixteenth century, the coif was worn beneath finer outer headwear, helping to secure the women's outer veils and headpieces that were pinned to it. In some portraits, the outer edge of the coif is clearly visible. Holbein's sketches are invaluable for the excellent information on different styles of coif, although it is sometimes difficult to tell if the outer edge is a trim on the hood, or, in fact, the coif itself.

Some coifs were wired at the front, as Holbein's sketch of Anne Boleyn shows. This style was possibly the type worn beneath a French hood, as the sides mirror the front shaping of the hoods that were fashionable at the time. There has been some debate as to whether the French hood was tied beneath the chin, but in this sketch, her coif looks to be fastened in this way. Another portrait that clearly illustrates a French hood tied beneath the chin is one by Holbein that was once thought to be Katherine Howard but now is open to debate.

Beneath Anne's coif in the portrait (see Plate 3) there is a glimpse of a separate hair covering, but its purposes are unclear. It could be a ribbon used to fasten her braided hair. The fabric wrapped around the head is unusual and the purpose unclear, but it could have been used to secure the hood in place.

As the period progressed, and the fashion moved away from the more cumbersome gable-style hood, the front of the hair became more visible. The coif itself was forced to change too, becoming smaller and more decorative. In some instances, as we move later into the period, portraiture suggests that no coif was worn at all.

As hoods became smaller, so did the coif. Among working-class women, they became a fashion item in themselves, developing different styles and shapes, and were clearly intended to be worn alone. Lace and embroidery were added to the bag coif (made with a gathered circle of linen to hold the hair at the back of the head) with attractive brim and side pieces. It gradually shifted further back on the head, revealing much more hair than had previously been acceptable. These coifs were similar to the one worn by Anne Boleyn in the image but were worn toward the back of the head. During the reign of Elizabeth I, who took extraordinary pride in her fabulous fiery red hair, the coif became so small, it was more of an embellishment to the hair than a means of concealing it.

The gabled hood (sometimes known as the English hood)

The terms 'gabled' and 'English' were first applied to this style of headwear by historical researchers. Contemporary accounts do not use the term. During the Tudor period, they were referred to simply as 'bonnet' and 'frontlet', making it difficult to determine which style the source is discussing.

One of the earliest examples of a 'gabled' hood can be seen in the portrait of Margaret Beaufort circa 1503 in which the frontlet is formed, either by starch or stiffener, into a point above her forehead. She has not a scrap of hair showing, and her plain white coif can be seen beneath the peak of the gable. Although Elizabeth of York wore a similar hood in her portrait, hers was more richly decorated compared with Margaret's stark, almost nun-like design. As the era progressed, this style evolved into the more elaborate, boxy shape favoured by Catherine of Aragon.

Again, we have Holbein to thank for his sketches and paintings of women of this period; without his observation, we'd have no idea as to the back view of a hood of this style. Although there are variations in decoration and the innovative methods of pinning the lapets (veils), there were very few changes in design throughout the Henrician period.

The gabled hood boasted lapets which were essentially two matching veils. These could either be left to hang down or pinned to the top. As time went on, the side lapets became shorter, ending at chin level. The front of the hair and the coif were hidden from view by striped silk fabric.

Figure 18: The author wearing her gabled hood. (*Photograph: J. Arnopp*)

This striped fabric element is described variously by re-enactors as a turban worn beneath the hood, or striped fabric sewn into the front of the hood, but we cannot be certain which is correct. Some researchers believe that in the earlier period at least, the 'turban' may in fact have been

Figure 19: The author's French hoods. (*Photograph: Judith Arnopp*)

their braided, wrapped hair showing, which later developed into a strip of fabric wrapped around the forehead.

The gabled hood was favoured by Catherine of Aragon, but the French style of hood replaced it in England shortly after Mary Tudor's (Henry VIII's sister) return from her brief sojourn as Queen of France. For some time, the two styles were worn side by side, but after Anne Boleyn came into favour and replaced Catherine of Aragon as queen, the French hood became the more fashionable option of the two.

The French hood was the more popular choice among the women of the court during Anne Boleyn's time as queen, but after her fall, her more conservative successor, Jane Seymour,

Figure 20: Mary Tudor, attributed to Jan Gossaert. (*Wikimedia Commons*)

banned the wearing of the French style and favoured the gabled style. Since headwear was an expensive item, the new rule caused problems for some members of the court. Lady Lisle, while fitting out her daughter to attend Queen Jane, had already paid out for French-style clothing before the new rules came into play. She was told,

> the queen's pleasure [is] that Mrs Anne shall wear out her French apparel, so that your ladyship shall thereby be no loser. Howbeit, she needs must have a bonnet of velvet and frontlet of the same. I saw her yesterday in her velvet bonnet that my lady Sussex had 'tired her in, and methought it became her nothing so well as the French hood; but the queen's pleasure must needs be fulfilled.[1]

But shortly afterwards, they received further instruction as to the style of bonnet which must have: 'frontlets and an edge of pearl, and a gown of black satin and another of velvet and this must be done before the queen's grace churching.'[2]

Tudor women, of course, were more accustomed to wearing hoods than we are, but I don't find them the easiest of things to wear. I never wear a hat in everyday life. I like the wind in my hair and a free flow of air around my head, but when I attend an event wearing my hood, because my ears are covered, sound is muted. Since I am also obliged to leave off my glasses, two of my senses are dulled, which makes it difficult to communicate. On the plus side, the gable hood is far more flattering to an ageing, wider face than the much smaller, lighter French hood, so I stick with it. I've also made a bongrace to go with my English gown, but I will discuss this further later on.

The French hood

The iconic Tudor French hood that we all love is having a makeover. During past decades, it has been depicted in film and television drama in many startling styles. Re-enactors, myself included, have religiously copied those styles, but our conception of the French hood is about to make a dramatic change.

Figure 21: Katherine Parr's tomb at Sudeley Castle. (*Photograph: Judith Arnopp*)

As early as 1516, Mary Tudor, sister to Henry VIII, is pictured wearing an early version of the French hood. As I mentioned before, she is believed to have brought the fashion to England on her return from her brief sojourn as Queen of France. There is no doubt its popularity increased further once Anne Boleyn returned from France, especially among the younger women of the court. The gabled style favoured by Catherine of Aragon did not die out completely, however, and the two styles continued to be worn in conjunction for some time.

Figure 22: Mary Brandon, Baroness of Monteagle, original sketch by Hans Holbein the Younger, author of the copy unknown. (*Wikimedia Commons*)

Early versions of the hood lay flat against the crown and framed the sides of the face, allowing for small areas of hair to show. It was a style that slowly evolved into what we now recognise as a French hood. It was rounded in shape, usually decorated with pearls and gold braid. The front was softened with a strip of pleated organza, sometimes white, sometimes gold or a combination of both. This style of hood sat further back on the head than the gable style and revealed the front of the hair, as can be seen in the 'Hever Portrait' of Anne Boleyn. The back of the hair was hidden from view, usually plaited, wrapped around, and fixed to the crown of the head, to be covered by the long veil, which was customarily made of black velvet. A decorated band or billament framed the face; this was made from velvet or taffeta and was pinned with jewels.

The hood part that hung down the back was usually black or red, and fashioned from velvet, taffeta, or silk. It is often claimed that modern-day re-enactors (myself included) are unauthentic if they wear a hood made from the same fabric as their gown, but there is one portrait of the young Elizabeth Tudor wearing a matching cap and gown, although it is red.

Figure 23: Eleanor of Austria (aged four), Meister der St Georgsgilde. (*Wikimedia Commons*)

No re-enactor today can achieve perfect authenticity; many of the fabrics, weaves and dyes are no longer available but, in our group, we strive to be as close as our budgets allow. However, it seems our interpretation for the French hood may have been incorrect all along and, if this is so, the hood was of far simpler construction than previously believed.

Recent independent studies by dress historians Samantha Bullat, Karen Margrethe Høskuldsson, and Dr Perin Westerhof Nyman have concluded that instead of being a one-piece item of headwear, the French hood may have been constructed by the layering of multiple parts. This three-part ensemble was made up of a white linen coif, a red silk cap, and a velvet hood with the brim turned back to reveal a contrasting silk lining.

They believe that the turned-back part of the outer hood has been mistaken in the past for a brim. The reason for this misinterpretation

Figure 24: Anne of Brittany by Jean Bourdichon. (*Wikimedia Commons*)

could be due to the perspective in some paintings which make the crescent appear to be standing vertical, proud of the head. Perhaps the artists intentionally distorted the perspective of the headwear to illustrate the hood's full glory, possibly at the request of the sitter – we will never know.

My interest piqued, I immediately scoured the internet and the books in my library for paintings and sculptures taken in profile and was excited to discover images of French hoods that do indeed illustrate the hood lying flat on the crown.

Like many others, I was completely shocked by this idea, but as soon as I saw Dr Perin Westerhof Nyman and Samantha Bullat's exceptionally beautiful replica three-part hoods, I was persuaded at once that it must have been so. I went straight to my sewing room to attempt to recreate my own.

I've been making French hoods in the old way for some time now. My early attempts with an old Simplicity pattern were awful. The crescent was far too high and, in my ignorance and often on the customer's request, I constructed them using fabric all the colours of the rainbow. As my skill and knowledge increased, I switched to the Tudor Tailor pattern, decreased the size of the crown, and reduced my range of colours, but I was excited to try yet another new method and one that makes so much more sense.

Images from the early part of the century make it clear that the front of the hood was indeed turned back, the folds in the fabric are easily detectable. But as the era progresses, the painting of the fold becomes smoother, less obvious, making it more difficult to determine how they are put together. Whether this is due to artistic representation alone, or a stylistic change in the hood itself, I can't be certain. One thing that is clear is that in the early period, the crown was flat to the head, there was no upstanding crescent as we see in modern films.[3] This flat crown style is especially evident in French portraits, which is, of course, the style of hood Anne Boleyn and Mary Tudor would have worn circa 1522.

The second layer, the red silk cap, was tight-fitting, fastening beneath the chin or tied to the plaited, coiled hair at the back. The front of the cap was decorated with a crimped gold organza (or similar) frill and sometimes had small embellishments along the edge. There has been some discussion as to whether the organza frill was attached to the linen coif or the cap, but some images clearly show the coif lies beneath the sheer gold trim. It may just have been the case that it varied depending on the taste of the wearer. The three-part hood seems to have been a very versatile item, folded and worn in a variety of ways.

In shape, it is assumed the under cap was similar to those from the late sixteenth and seventeenth century, with a fold at the top of the head, a gathered crown, with a back seam, and casing along the lower edge to house the drawstring. This string would have been white, either sewn to one side of the chin and pinned to the other, or alternatively, a cord run through a back casing and secured to the plaited and coiled hair to give that lovely Tudor shape to the back of the head.

The veil (hood) was almost always black velvet, cut in one piece with a fold on top of the head with the veil, shaped like a tube, extending from the back. It was often satin lined, and the edge that lined the face usually embellished with gold beads or pearls.

Close examination of the portrait of Anne Boleyn suggests she may be wearing a black coif with a gold organza-trimmed cap. There is the suggestion of a chin strap on the cap and the paste crescent is of black pearl-trimmed velvet.

To help keep the hood in place, the hair was taped and bound to the back of the head and covered with the coif. The cap was then placed on top, the draw string wrapping around the braided and coiled hair to provide stability. The front of the hood was folded back and then back on itself again to display the jewelled edge. I strongly advise you search out Samantha Bullat, Karen Margrethe Høskuldsson, and Dr Perin Westerhof Nyman's YouTube videos for visual clarification.

Later in the period, the French hood evolved further to include a 'paste' attached to the cap. This was made of silk- or velvet-covered paste buckram and sometimes wired. If we accept this three-part French hood theory, the outer hood itself remained unchanged, fitting over the cap and paste. In this later period, the hood was folded back further to reveal more of the silk lining, although in some cases, to make things more difficult to interpret, the hood and lining were made of the same fabric, increasing our confusion as to how the whole thing was assembled.

Another new addition was the billament – a separate piece, shaped to fit around the head to frame the face, embellished with jewels. This was a separate element and likely to have been interchangeable to create different looks for different events.

Samantha Bullat stresses that this new hypothesis may be wrong; we are, after all, constantly experimenting and reconsidering the past and how things were done, but to me, her theory makes far more sense than the traditional interpretation.

As yet, I have only made two prototypes. Before I splash out on costly fabric and embellishments, I want to wear it around the house for a while to iron out any changes that might be necessary. For me, even though this theory cannot yet be proven to be accurate, it is the most exciting idea I've yet come across.

Figure 25: Anne Boleyn 'Hever Portrait' showing a lot of hair, wearing a trimmed cap with pearl-edged paste, English school. (*Wikimedia Commons*)

I am not the most elegant of women. I've worn a French hood many times and I have found it difficult to keep it in place without copious pinning. Even with a coif, it tends to slide from the back of my head, or I displace it by knocking the hard prominent crescent on something. With the new style, I suffered none of those inconveniences.

Figure 26: The author's three-layered French hood. (*Photograph: Judith Arnopp*)

Of course, royal women were expected to do very little while wearing their court clothes – if they wanted something fetching, they sent a servant. If they dropped something, there was always somebody nearby to retrieve it for them. I've only attempted the early version and not yet tried the paste and fancy billament, and I've cheated by lining the red cap with white linen and adding the pleated organza to that, so my version is in fact only two layers, but so far, I am impressed. As long as you have your braided hair pinned in the correct position, the hood stays on! I did not bash it on things, and it required far fewer pins.

During the Elizabethan period, the hood evolved further, becoming smaller and worn even further back on the head. Elizabeth was proud of her pretty red hair and showed it off as much as possible, wearing it dressed in rolls or curls. Her women copied the new style until eventually the fashion became more focused on the hair itself than the covering headwear.

The stickelchen cap

Hans Holbein the Younger's portrait of Anne of Cleves shows her wearing a 'stickelchen cap' – a style of headwear that is not really considered 'Tudor', since Anne and Henry's marriage was so quickly annulled, and she adopted a style that was more fashionable in England. In my opinion, the stickelchen cap is more flattering than the gabled hood and prettier than the French style, so I thought it worth a mention here.

Figure 27: Anne of Cleves miniature by Hans Holbein the Younger. (*Wikimedia Commons*)

The name 'stickelchen' is taken from a label on one of Albrecht Durer's sketches. It appears to have originated in the Cologne area. Like the French hood, it was made up of several layers beginning with a forehead cloth, a wide band of embroidered silk that was wrapped around the head. On top of this, Anne is wearing a fine, sheer linen under cap that resembles the Dutch caps of later national costume with the sides folded back to form wings.

To help maintain its distinct shape, the 'stickelchen' probably had a buckram inner, which was covered with silk and decorated with embroidery and jewels. Barthelomaeus Bruyn portraits provide some of the best examples of this style of cap. I haven't yet experimented with sewing this style, but it is on my exceptionally long to-do list.

Bongrace

Another form of Tudor headwear is the 'bongrace' (see the lady on the right in Figure 59). This was a plain, unembellished style of hood worn with the veil flipped up and over the head, sometimes forming a peak. It can be made from linen or lightweight wool or for upper classes, velvet, or silk. In the image, the lady wearing an orange or russet English gown sports a lovely bongrace. Pictorial evidence for this style is very rare but there are several carved examples in churches of the period. The Gerard family

Figure 28: The tomb of the Gerard family, showing the women in bongrace bonnets. (*Wikimedia Commons*)

memorial at the church of St John the Baptist, Ashley, in Staffordshire, depicts Sir Gilbert Gerard, his son Thomas (1st Baron Gerard) and his four daughters, Frances, Radclyffe, Catherine, and Margaret. The women are all wearing bongrace caps.

Partlet

A partlet was a short garment covering the upper chest and shoulders and secured beneath the arms by ties or pins. Some examples, particularly from the latter part of the era, have a high collar, others a rounded neck. Worn by both men and women of all strata of society, they came in a range of fabric.

The upper classes preferred velvet or silk with a fine linen lining; they were often black, particularly earlier in the period, later evolving to a sheer fabric. When viewing portraits from this era, it is sometimes difficult to spot the partlet, as the fashion was to have them made from the same fabric as the gown. What we immediately presume to be a high-necked

Figure 29: Elizabeth I, *The Pelican Portrait*, by Nicholas Hilliard. (*Wikimedia Commons*)

gown is in fact a traditional French-style gown worn with a matching high-necked partlet.

The lower echelons wore partlets of wool and linen. Initially the garment was worn over the gown but at some point, this changed, and by the Elizabethan era, it was worn beneath the kirtle but over the corset.

Figure 30: Working woman in kirtle and partlet. (*Photograph: J. Arnopp*)

By then, for the upper classes at least, it had evolved into something rather more decorative than functional. There are examples of partlets made of fine lawn or lace, and they are worn in numerous ways, too. Sometimes they are closed at the top, and open at the bottom, as in the Pelican portrait of Elizabeth I in which she wears a fine black worked partlet with a high neck, worn with a small ruff. The higher collar on the partlet served as a barrier between the skin and the ruff, not only protecting the ruff from sweat and dirt but also providing an anchoring point for the many pins the ruff required.

Gloves

Gloves have been an essential part of the wardrobe since time began, the earliest pair having been found in Tutankhamun's tomb. Early styled gloves would have served practical purposes rather than fashion, but after the Norman conquest in England, gloves became a badge of distinction, worn by nobles and dignitaries. By the time of the Tudors, they were a high fashion item, embroidered and embellished to enhance an already flamboyant outfit. Gloves made a statement and can be seen in many portraits, either worn or held in the hand to indicate the sitter was *en vogue*.

They were made from leather, silk, linen, or lace. Like everything else, they were embroidered, embellished with pearls, emeralds, rubies, or sapphires. They were beribboned, tasselled, and fringed. As far as the Tudors were concerned, the fancier the gloves, and the less practical, the better they were. Elizabeth I held them in high favour, and it became customary at New Year for members of the court to present the queen with gloves; she is said to have owned more than two thousand pairs.

At a ceremony in Oxford in 1566, there is a report of the queen being presented with an eighteen-inch pair of leather gauntlets with two inches of gold fringing. These are now housed at the Ashmolean Museum in Oxford and reveal how dainty the queen's hands must have been and how long her fingers. The queen was famous for her exquisite hands and during audiences, she would remove her gloves to show off, not just the beauty of her gloves, but that of her hands.

Gloves were an intimate gift between lovers, a gift that was never given lightly but presented only to those you wished to impress. The glove became so symbolic of status that it was 'thrown down' as a challenge, as a mark of affront. But it could also be used as a mark of favour. George Clifford, 3rd Earl of Cumberland, was the queen's champion and is depicted in a portrait by Nicholas Hilliard, dressed in his tilting clothes. A closer look reveals he has one of the queen's diamond-encrusted gloves pinned to his hat, as a sign of her favour.

Of course, there were also working gloves, and gauntlets worn by falconers and knights. Gloves, being an integral part of the costumes that we are endeavouring to represent, should be a vital ingredient of any re-enactor's wardrobe, but they are not easy to make and accurate examples are expensive to purchase. If anyone questions my bare hands, I usually pretend to have carelessly left my gloves somewhere and send a servant off in search of them.

Embroidery

As you will by now have realised, the later Tudors, the upper classes at least, embellished every garment they possibly could, and this included their undies. The collar and cuffs of shifts and chemises, the sleeves and front edge of a man's shirt – any piece of fabric that would be on show (and sometimes garments that wouldn't be seen) was embellished.

It is often claimed that Catherine of Aragon introduced blackwork embroidery to England but in Chaucer's *Canterbury Tales*, which was written around 1387, the clothes of the Miller's Wife are described: 'of white, too, was the dainty smock she wore, embroidered at the collar all about with coal-black silk, alike within and out',[4] thus proving that blackwork was clearly worn in England much earlier than the sixteenth century.

Due to its association with Catherine, for many years, the blackwork style of embroidery was known as 'Spanish work'. There is little doubt the style grew in popularity during her reign, but the technique actually originated in Africa, probably arriving in Spain during the time of the Moors. After Henry VIII set Catherine aside in favour of Anne Boleyn, all references to Catherine as queen were discouraged, and attempts were made to erase her presence from the palace. As Henry's relationship with Spain soured, the former queen's favourite style of embroidery, although not becoming less popular, was henceforth known simply as 'blackwork'.

There are scarcely any early blackworked garments left in existence. The examples we do have are merely fragments or pieces of clothing where the blackwork thread has rotted away, but the tiny holes left by the needle reveal the ghost of a once splendid design. The reason they have perished is due to the dyeing process of the silk. There are some such examples of blackwork from the sixteenth and seventeenth centuries in

Figure 31: Henry VIII of England, by Hans Holbein. (*Wikimedia Commons*)

the Victoria and Albert Museum in London. A few pieces remain where the embroidery appears to be brown instead of black and this fading too is due to home-produced dyes. Again, we have Holbein to thank for recording in his portraits and sketches the exquisite detail of Tudor blackwork and many other aspects of Tudor fashion.

Due to the stitch counting required, this style of embroidery was mostly applied to even weave fabrics, fine linen, or silk but also satin and velvet. Geometric shapes were favoured on collars and cuffs, but more fluid motifs were also popular. In the portrait shown on the previous page (Figure 31), Henry VIII sports a gorgeous blackworked shirt, embroidered with a swirling floral design of acanthus leaves.

The stitches were often, but not always, counted, a method in which the fabric threads are counted before the needle is inserted into the fabric. This requires a keen eye and a great deal of patience. There are several different stitches, a double running stitch as depicted on collars and cuffs in so many of Holbein's Tudor court portraits that has come to be known to dress historians as the Holbein stitch. This was the preferred stitch for areas of the garment where both sides would be visible, as it is supposed to be identical, back and front. Unfortunately, my own attempts at it never are.

Stem stitch is an outline stitch used in the geometric blackwork as illustrated on Henry's shirt in the portrait discussed previously. For added texture to either style of embroidery, braid or plaited stitches were used to raise the design.

Blackwork was not restricted to clothing but was used on bed linen and cushions also. Although, in a professional sense, embroidery was carried out by men, women enjoyed it too. Court women spent many hours waiting on the queen; hours that could be tedious and long and, since embroidery is easily portable and can be put down and picked up again at will, it became a favoured pastime.

Catherine of Aragon, as mentioned before, was a skilled needlewoman and took pride in embroidering the king's shirts, continuing to do so even after he had shunned her for the younger, more vibrant Anne Boleyn. She passed on the skill to her daughter, Princess Mary, who also excelled at the art. Princess Elizabeth too displayed a talent for embroidery beyond her years, as she did in most things.

By the time Elizabeth came to rule, blackwork had altered in style, becoming less rigid and far more fluid and symbolic. Sometimes gold and silver thread was used alongside the black silk and occasional seed pearls were sewn into the design. During this time, the coif had ceased to be worn by men but continued to be used as a covering for a woman's hair. But plain coifs or even simple blackworked edgings were a thing of the past and the embroidered embellishment became far more elaborate. Floral motifs were preferred, largely due to the symbolic significance of flowers, as Jen Goodwin notes in her book, *Blackwork Embroidery: Techniques and Projects.*

> Daisies were known for innocence, roses for love, pansies for thoughts, honeysuckle for devotion and holly for foresight, to mention a few. Other common elements were oak for steadfastness (acorns represented strength and potential), pears for fertility and abundance, and pomegranates for resurrection and chastity.[5]

The importance of symbolism peaked during Elizabeth's reign, and almost every portrait of her is replete with coded messages that only those in the know could decipher. Most famous is the Rainbow Portrait, which can be viewed at her childhood home in Hatfield. Painted between 1600 and 1602, Elizabeth was in her sixties, yet she appears to be ageless. She is dressed in a fine linen bodice, embroidered with colourful spring flowers, a mantle is draped over her left shoulder, and beneath an extravagant headdress, her hair is loose, to depict her virginal state. Her cloak is embroidered with ears and eyes, illustrating that she hears and sees all. The serpent of wisdom is coiled about her left arm, and in her hand, she clutches a rainbow with the Latin motto that translates as 'no rainbow without the sun'.

As this portrait shows, other more colourful forms of embroidery were increasing in popularity. For the re-enactor, however, blackwork is relatively easy to achieve, or at least, a facsimile of the style.

Blackwork is relatively simple to learn. If you have a good eye and a steady hand, it is possible to learn to replicate simple designs quite quickly. As your skill improves, you may even find the more intricate styles achievable. For those who can't or have no wish to, there are printed fabrics available, but they come at a cost. I have used both methods in the past, but although I enjoyed the close work of counted stitches, the freer style was easier and just as effective. Period cross-stitch pattern charts are available online. You can either use the counted method or use a lightbox to trace the design onto the fabric using a soluble pen. It is then just a case of stitching neatly over the lines.

Alternatively, an easier way around it is to purchase the printed fabric and stitch over that. From a distance, I'd defy anyone to notice.

The clothes of Henry VIII's queens

A lady's clothes marked her place in society. The quality of cloth, the volume necessary and the embellishment upon it immediately revealed her status, and her worth as well as her sense of style. Queen Catherine of Aragon wore plain clothes in private 'as a sign of humility'[6] but in public she dressed as sumptuously as the king. She favoured the Spanish style, choosing purple, black, and crimson, which were among the most difficult dyes to achieve. She preferred velvet, satin, and tilsent, and when the occasion warranted, she wore cloth of gold and pearls – yet beneath this it is believed she wore the habit of St Francis to mark her piety. It is interesting to note that Catherine's expenditure on clothing averaged around £700–£800 per annum but for the years 1526–1527 it leapt to £1,152 – coinciding with Henry's growing infatuation with Anne Boleyn and indicating perhaps a desperate attempt on Catherine's part to win back her husband.

On her return from the French court, Anne Boleyn is well known for her introduction of fresh new styles of dress. She was not described as a great beauty, yet most contemporaries noted her wit and style. In 1528, a Venetian diplomat wrote that Anne was: 'Not one of the handsomest women in the world; she is of middling stature, swarthy complexion, long neck, wide mouth, a bosom not much raised and eyes which are black and beautiful.'

In the sixteenth century, George Wyatt, grandson and biographer of the Tudor courtier and one time admirer of Anne, Thomas Wyatt, wrote of Anne: 'Albeit in beauty she was to many inferior, but for behaviour, manners, attire and tongue she excelled them all, for she had been brought up in France.'

Which clearly illustrates that even then, style had very little to do with beauty. There are indications in the record that suggest Anne not only wore clothes of the latest fashion but added her own tweaks and dashes of ingenuity that made her stand out from other women. Nicholas Sanders, who was no friend to Anne, stated: 'She was the model and the mirror of those who were at court, for she was always well-dressed, and every day made some change in the fashion of her garments.'[7]

She favoured bright colours, gold and yellow, and also fur. A record for December 1530 notes that monies were paid to Adington the skinner for furs for her gowns. There are also receipts of crimson cloth of gold, and in 1532, a black satin night gown. This 'night gown' was not a garment for sleeping in as we think of it today but a comfortable gown to be worn in the evenings.

Once the king had determined to make Anne his wife, in order to raise her to marriageable status, Henry created her Marquis of Pembroke in her own right. For the ceremony, she wore ermine-trimmed crimson velvet. For her coronation, she chose a violet velvet mantle with a high ruff of gold thread and pearls.

Anne's replacement, Jane Seymour, is usually viewed as a meeker, simpler woman than Anne, displaying less wit than her predecessor and more compassion. She was married to the king just eleven days after Anne's execution. Jane was of the old school, more in the mould of Catherine both in manner and dress. Like Catherine, she was deeply religious, clinging to the Catholic faith. At 27 or 28, she was past the usual age for marriage and made sure she dressed to her best advantage. Jane, disliking the French hood which Anne had favoured, turned the fashion at court back to the gable style. This could have been her way of snubbing Anne and marking allegiance to Catherine but could also point to the realisation that the gable was more flattering to her wide face.

Jane's wardrobe included a wider range of garments in a broader range of colours than Henry's first queen. She favoured velvet and satin; her accounts include payments for crimson satin for the bodice of a velvet kirtle and purple satin for the bodice of a purple velvet kirtle.

Of all the royal portraits of Henry's wives, my favourite is Hans Holbein the Younger's portrait of Jane Seymour. To modern tastes, she isn't the prettiest of women, but fashions change over time and what we find attractive, Henry would find the opposite. Interestingly, her appearance doesn't match the descriptions of the meek creature we often read about. There is a decisive set to her jaw and her eyes are confident, but it isn't really Jane's appearance or character that interests me, it is what she is wearing.

She has the most exquisite sleeves, with delicately embroidered cuffs, and the fabric of her gown has been painted so perfectly the viewer knows that if they were to reach out and touch the gown, the velvet would be smooth and soft. Of Jane's many pairs of sleeves, forty-nine were decorated with aglets of gold with embroidery to match. One pair of her sleeves were decorated with the king's initials, worked in gold. In her portrait, she is wearing the gable style of hood, with one lapet pinned up, the other down. If you zoom in really close, tiny wisps of hair are visible, peeking from beneath the striped silk 'turban' which, in this portrait, appears to be part of the hood rather than a separate garment.

Jane had a position to maintain, and since clothing has always been the best way to issue a statement, she is quite possibly attempting to adopt some of her predecessor's glamour. Jane was queen for such a brief time that if it weren't for Holbein's portrait, we would probably have no idea what she looked like. Thankfully, he has made such a detailed likeness that we can learn a vast amount from the one painting.

Where the tastes and fashions of Henry's first three queens were adopted by the court, his fourth queen was forced to amend her own style to fit in with English fashion. Anne of Cleves put off the clothes favoured in her own country and adopted those currently popular in England.

To strengthen his position against France and the Holy Roman Empire, Henry, or rather Cromwell, desired a match with one of the sisters of William of Cleves. Undecided whether to choose Anne or her sister, Amelia, ambassadors were sent to Cleves to assess the suitability of each. When the two women were presented, they appeared in what was described as 'monstrous habit and apparel'.

Holbein's portrait of Anne, however, was pleasing to the king and persuaded Henry to select her as his bride. To Cromwell's delight, Anne was shipped off to England, escorted by female attendants who were 'clothed like herself – a thing which looks strange to many'.[8]

In Cleves at the time, women favoured Netherlandish fashions with high necks and wide puffed sleeves. When he met her, Henry was not enamoured of his new wife but, forced to go through with the ceremony,

Figure 32: Anne of Cleves by Hans Holbein the Younger. (*Public domain, Wikimedia Commons*)

he did so with little grace and, immediately afterward, charged Thomas Cromwell to find a way to free him from it.

Many reasons for Henry's reluctance to marry Anne have been put forward, not least her appearance and noxious odour, but of all the queens' portraits, I find Anne of Cleves to be the most attractive. There are various reasons why Henry failed to notice Anne's good points. Impatient to meet his new bride, shortly after she disembarked, Henry set off from court to surprise her at Rochester. The Spanish ambassador reported the incident:

> And on New Year's Day in the afternoon the king's grace with five of his privy chamber, being disguised with mottled cloaks with hoods so that they should not be recognised, came secretly to Rochester, and so went up into the chamber where the said Lady Anne was looking out of a window to see the bull-baiting which was going on in the courtyard, and suddenly he embraced and kissed her, and showed her a token which the king had sent her for a New Year's gift, and she being abashed and not knowing who it was thanked him, and so he spoke with her. But she regarded him little, but always looked out the window ... and when the king saw that she took so little notice of his coming he went into another chamber and took off his cloak and came in again in a coat of purple velvet. And when the lords and knights saw his grace they did him reverence ... and then her grace humbled herself lowly to the king's majesty, and his grace saluted her again, and they talked together lovingly, and afterwards he took her by the hand and led her to another chamber where their graces amused themselves that night and on Friday until the afternoon.[9]

This was all part of the courtly love tradition that the king so loved to play. There was nothing Henry loved more than to disguise himself and surprise his subjects when he revealed his true identity. Anne was supposed to swoon with pleasure at the enthusiastic arrival of her soon to be spouse but her failure to understand this, and her obvious lack of delight at her future husband's sudden appearance, quite possibly sealed her fate. Henry was used to being adored and his disappointment in Anne's response made it impossible for him to forgive her. Anne, to be fair, had just suffered a difficult voyage and probably just wanted time to recuperate. She understood no, or very little, English and was unschooled in court customs. She was also expecting the king to be the virile, handsome prince the ambassadors reported him to be. She would have seen his splendid portrait, but by the time of their first meeting, Henry was ageing, putting on weight, and already suffering from a malodorous leg injury. It is likely she was more disappointed than he was, but Henry set out to rid himself of her and in doing so derided her appearance, her personal hygiene and even her morality. 'She is nothing fair, and have very evil smells about her,' and, adding insult to injury, he also, 'plainly mistrusted her to be no maid by reason of the looseness of her belly and breasts and other tokens.'

But other reports differ and some are complimentary, and illustrate that Anne had a great love of clothes and had no qualms about adopting the style of dress popular in England at that time.

> Then the Lordes went to fetche the Ladye Anne, whiche was apparelled in a gowne of ryche cloth of gold set full of large flowers of great & Orient Pearle, made after the Dutche fassion rownde, her here hangyng downe, whych was fayre, yelowe and long: On her head a Coronall of gold replenished with great stone, and set about full of braunches of Rosemary, about her necke and middle, luelles of great valew & estimacion.[10]

Shortly after the wedding, the chronicler, Edward Hall, reported that Anne was dressed in the English fashion, wearing a French hood that Hall declared, 'so set forth her beauty and good visage that every creature rejoiced to behold her'.

It is unfortunate that Henry took such a dislike to Anne, but she appears to have accepted Henry's suggestion of an annulment with as much compliance as she accepted the marriage proposal. Given the circumstances, compared with his other wives, Anne did very well indeed. She not only kept her head but was granted an income, with clothes, jewels, and a household to match her status. On top of this, she was granted many properties including Richmond Palace and Hever Castle. In return, Anne promised that after the annulment she would commit herself wholly to king and country and to 'remain his servant and subject'.[11]

Of course, she must have experienced some level of humiliation at being rejected by the king of England. Perhaps her willingness to accept the annulment was to disguise her shame at being found unsuitable, perhaps she was simply relieved not to have to sleep with the king any longer. But there are hints that she may after all have had ambition. After her successor Katherine Howard's fall, Anne gave indications that she would welcome a remarriage with the king, but it wasn't to be. She remained on very friendly terms with the king and remained part of court life where she was given precedence over the court women, her status second only to the king's wife and sister.

Often in debt, Anne failed to spend much on the maintenance of her properties, but the French ambassador noted that Anne 'wears new dresses every day'. Perhaps that is where her income went. I think we can all relate to that.

During Henry and Edward's reign, Anne attended functions as an honorary member of the royal family, known as 'the king's beloved sister'. Anne was very close in age to Princess Mary and the two formed a close friendship. She was given a position of honour at Mary's own coronation in 1553 and although there was some suspicion of her involvement in Wyatt's rebellion in 1554, nothing was proven, and she and the queen remained friendly until Anne's death in 1557. She was buried in Westminster Abbey with full honour to befit her status as former queen and 'beloved sister' of Henry VIII.

In a wildly inaccurate chronicle of Henry VIII known as *The Spanish Chronicle*, it was stated, 'The King had no wife who made him spend so much money in dresses and jewels as she did, who every day had some fresh caprice.'

The wife the author was referring to was Katherine Howard; the tragic young woman of whom we know so little apart from that she was very beautiful, vivacious, and fatally promiscuous. The king was wildly enamoured of his young wife and, as if in attempt to keep old age at bay, he showered her with gifts of land, jewellery, and rich textiles. It might be an assumption that she was as obsessive as most young women over clothes and fashion, but there are hints in her story as to her generosity and exuberance, which sits well with a passion for fine things.

When Henry made Katherine a gift of two spaniels, she impulsively passed one to her predecessor, Anne of Cleves, with whom she was good friends. She also gave Anne the gift of a valuable ring. Later, when she was queen and learned of Margaret Pole, the Countess of Salisbury's imprisonment in the Tower, there was nothing Katherine could do to secure her release. Instead, she sent the old lady a furred nightgown, a furred petticoat, a kirtle, a nightgown, a frontlet, four pairs of hose, four pairs of shoes, and one pair of slippers. But Katherine's affection was not enough to sway the king's decision and Margaret Pole was beheaded in a grisly fashion a few weeks later.

Margaret was not the only family member to benefit from Katherine's generosity. She also made Princess Mary and Elizabeth gifts of jewellery. Perhaps Katherine was delighted to be queen and wanted to share her good fortune, or perhaps she was attempting to buy the approval of her stepchildren, who were both grown women. Unfortunately, these brief glimpses into the character of Katherine Howard are all we have; we are not even certain if the portrait purporting to be her has been correctly attributed.

Judging by her clothes, the sitter in question is likely to be a queen, or a lady of very high rank (see Figure 33). The jewel she wears is also depicted in an earlier portrait of Jane Seymour, which strengthens the claim the sitter could be Katherine wearing inherited royal jewels. Later in Henry's reign, his sixth and final wife, Katherine Parr, was also painted wearing the same jewel.

Recently, it has been suggested that the sitter isn't Katherine Howard but Anne of Cleves, and when you compare the portrait with the miniature painted by Holbein prior to Henry's marriage with Anne, there are some convincing likenesses. The eye shape is similar, as is the tilt of the chin, and the shape of the brows. As I said before, the jewels point

Figure 33: Miniature of Katherine Howard by Hans Holbein the Younger. (*Wikimedia Commons*)

to the portrait being one of Henry's queens. The portrait is dated to or close to 1540, a year in which there were two queens, Anne of Cleves, and Katherine Howard. So, we can be confident it is one or the other.

Since we have a confirmed portrait of Anne with which to compare it, my vote is that it is Anne, not Katherine, either that or the two women were remarkably similar. There are no surviving records of Katherine having been painted, which bolsters the argument for it being Anne, but if it is so then it is a great shame that we have no clues as to Katherine's appearance.

We know Katherine championed the French style of gown, and the court followed suit, discarding their gable hoods once again in favour of the French. There are few references to her clothes, although we know they mattered to her. During the early days of courtship, Henry gave her '23 lengths of quilted sarcenet'[12] and later, in 1541, a billament of diamonds and rubies. Later that same year, when she was arrested for adultery and treason, her clothes and jewels were removed to mark her lost status.

In the months leading up to her execution, she was allowed only six French hoods with goldsmith work but no stones or pearls; six pairs of sleeves, six gowns, and six kirtles in satin, damask, and velvet. While this might seem a generous number of gowns to us, when you consider how many she would have owned as queen, to be allowed only six was punishment indeed.

While Katherine was imprisoned at Syon House, awaiting execution, the Spanish ambassador reported that she was 'taking great care to be well apparelled and more imperious and troublesome to serve than ever she was with the king'.[13]

She arrived at the Tower on the tenth day of February 1541, dressed modestly in black velvet, but we don't know what she chose to wear for her execution three days later. It is nice to think that perhaps, like her cousin Anne, she wore red for martyrdom and ermine as a sign of royalty, in a last silent but defiant statement of her innocence and status. But, unlike Anne, of course, Katherine was probably guilty of the accusations against her. She loved unwisely, ridiculed the king, and that is why she died. Afterward, Henry was reportedly grief-stricken and wept openly before the court, a broken and hopeless old man. But he didn't remain so for long.

In her youth, Katherine Parr's mother, Maud Green, was lady-in-waiting to Catherine of Aragon, and the queen stood as Katherine's godmother at her christening. This close association between the two makes it quite likely that Henry's last queen was named in honour of his first.

Henry was not Katherine's first husband. She had been previously wed at the age of 17 to Sir Edward Burgh and, after his death, to John Neville, 3rd Baron Latimer. He died in 1543 and during her widowhood, she formed an attachment to Sir Thomas Seymour, brother to the late queen, Jane. When King Henry proposed marriage to Katherine, there was little she could do but terminate her relationship with Seymour, who was dispatched on an overseas posting, and agree to marry the king.

Katherine entered marriage with Henry perfectly aware of the fate of his previous wives yet gave no indication of fear. Katherine was an intelligent, educated woman, keen for the new learning, and published several books on the subject. She fulfilled her royal duties well and was trusted enough to undertake the role of regent during Henry's campaign in France. She received praise for the manner in which she ran the country during his absence. Not only was she intelligent but also attractive and stylish, making careful adjustments to her clothes once she became queen, illustrating that she was aware of the importance of her new royal image.

In 1544, she was described by de Gante, the secretary to the Duke of Najera:

> She is of a lively and pleasing appearance and is praised as a virtuous woman. She was dressed in a robe of cloth of gold and a petticoat of brocade with sleeves lined with crimson satin and trimmed with three-piled crimson velvet. Her train was more than two yards long. Suspended from her neck were two crosses, and a jewel of very rich diamonds and in her head-dress were many and beautiful ones. Her girdle was of gold with large pendants.

There are several portraits of Katherine, including a full-length one taken around 1545 by Master John. In this, she wears a gown of cloth of silver tissue with a repeat pomegranate design. It has a tight fitted bodice with a squared neckline, the bodice ending in a point at the waist. Beneath, although it can't be seen, she has a farthingale which provides the conical shape to the skirts.

In a half portrait painted around the same time by William Scrots, she is wearing a masculine-style cap over her coif, decorated with pearls and a jaunty feather. Her heavily embroidered gown appears to be made of crimson satin. It has an upstanding collar in the English style, with a looser fitting bodice pleated and possibly cinched at the waist. The sleeves are very full, embroidered with geometric gold thread in vertical bands.

Katherine favoured crimson and gold; this combination of colours is mentioned several times in the records, and later during her time as queen, she also wore purple. She seems to have had a passion for shoes, ordering them in many colours, trimmed with gold, costing fourteen shillings a pair. There are cordwainers' bills that list the quantity of shoes she ordered. One pair of buskins, fifty-six pairs of shoes. Thirty-two pairs for the Maundy, two pairs of walking shoes, four pairs of lined shoes, four pairs lined and corked, two pairs, low voided shoes, two pairs of slippers, four pairs of lined slippers – that was just for the year between July 1543 and August 1544. She ordered a further forty-seven pairs in the following year. Imelda Marcos, eat your heart out!

She was as generous as her predecessor and made gifts of clothing to Prince Edward, Princess Mary, Princess Elizabeth, and Anne of Cleves. Deliveries were made several times a month to the queen, including silk ribbon, lengths of velvet, sarcenet, gloves, tassels, and caps. She also received large quantities of silk from the silk house at Whitehall, again in her favourite hues of crimson and purple.

After Henry's death in 1547, Katherine, as dowager, moved to her house in Chelsea with the young Princess Elizabeth. Shortly afterwards, she married a man of her own choosing, her old flame, Thomas Seymour, but it was a marriage that was to prove both short and tragic. Just one year after the king's death, Katherine died at Sudeley Castle, shortly after giving birth to Seymour's daughter. Seymour was executed for treason against his nephew, Edward VI, in February 1549.

After her death, clothing belonging to Katherine was removed from Sudeley and returned to Whitehall. Although there was no mention of gowns or kirtles, the array of partlets, placards, sleeves and caps were of the very finest quality, and almost all decorated with metallic embroidery, cutwork, and many aglets. The main fabrics used were velvet, cloth of silver, and satin in shades of purple, crimson, and black.

Although she was queen for just four years, Katherine was Henry's second-longest lasting wife, and we know more about her taste in clothes than we do of Henry's other queens. There are two very good contemporary portraits which allow us to see her face, the books she wrote provide access to her spiritual beliefs, and her clothing accounts provide invaluable information regarding her shopping habits, her style, her favourite colours and fabrics. We even have a swatch of her burial gown and a lock of her hair taken from her coffin in the eighteenth century.

Because more records survive detailing the expenditure of Henry's first and last queens, it doesn't necessarily mean they spent more of their allowance on clothes than the other four women, it simply points to the possibility of records being lost over time.

Elizabeth Tudor – Princess and Queen

Elizabeth was just two years and eight months old at the time of her mother Anne Boleyn's execution in 1536. It is probable that she didn't recall or miss her mother; the memory of the bright, exquisitely dressed visitor to her nursery at Hatfield in Hertfordshire would have faded very quickly. Elizabeth continued to reside there under the care of Lady Bryan until she was replaced by Catherine Champernowne/Ashley who remained Elizabeth's companion throughout her life. The infant Elizabeth would have been unaware of the significance of her reduced status from Princess of England to royal bastard, but she would have noticed drastic changes in the way she was treated. In fact, since her situation was unprecedented, it may be that those in charge of her had no idea of the etiquette for such a situation. Lady Bryan wrote to Cromwell on several occasions asking for clarification. The first record we have regarding Elizabeth's well-being are requests to Cromwell to provide clothing.

I beg you to be good to her and hers, and that she may have raiment, for she has neither gown nor kirtle, nor petticoat, nor linen for smocks, no kerchiefs, sleeves, rails, body stitchets, handkerchiefs, mufflers, not begins. All thys her Graces mostake I have dreven of as long as I can, that be my throthe, I cannot drive it any longer.[14]

This has often been interpreted as neglect on the king's part but since similar letters were later written on behalf of Prince Edward's wardrobe,

Figure 34: Princess Elizabeth Tudor, attributed to Scrots. (*Wikimedia Commons*)

whom Henry would never neglect, I think it was just a case of a growth spurt and mishandling of the situation by the council. The letter was written just a few weeks after Anne's death, and we know that the late queen kept Elizabeth well supplied with all she needed as a royal princess. It is unlikely she would have outgrown or worn out her clothes so quickly.

It may have been the case that Lady Bryan was trying to keep the council aware of Elizabeth's existence and requirements.

Even as a child, Elizabeth was extremely intelligent, diligent at her lessons, and there is nothing to suggest she was unhappy. More than one of her four stepmothers went out of their way to embrace her into the royal family and ease her into the king's good graces.

After the king's death, Elizabeth accompanied Katherine Parr to Chelsea, where the Dowager Queen lived until her marriage to Thomas Seymour. During this period, Elizabeth first encountered the dangers of being born too close to the throne. Her new stepfather, widely reputed to be dashing and handsome, took an unhealthy interest in Elizabeth,

Figure 35: Thomas Seymour by Nicolas Denisot. (*Public domain, Wikimedia Commons*)

teasing and tickling her inappropriately. When Mistress Ashley took her concerns to Katherine Parr, who incidentally was pregnant with Seymour's child by this time, the Dowager Queen dismissed his actions as horseplay.

After that, Katherine began to accompany Seymour when he burst into Elizabeth's room. There is even a bewildering account of him taking a dislike to a black gown Elizabeth was wearing and cutting it to ribbons while she was still wearing it. As Katherine's pregnancy advanced, Seymour's attention to Elizabeth increased until the dowager could no longer ignore the situation and, accusing Elizabeth of disloyalty, had her sent away. Elizabeth, who professed her innocence, withdrew to Cheshunt with her reputation in tatters.

It is very difficult not to judge this situation from a twenty-first century perspective. There is no doubt that Seymour was wrong to dally with his wife's ward, and there is no doubt that Elizabeth was wrong to indulge it. But in a sixteenth-century context, I don't think we should view it as child abuse. Elizabeth was of marriageable age; the real sin was dallying with a girl of royal blood, illegitimate or not. He should have known better, but Elizabeth was a teenager and would not have been the first to form an inappropriate infatuation for an older man. There is much more to this story, which continues after Katherine Parr's death, when Seymour, assisted by Catherine Ashley, attempted to form a marriage between him and the young Elizabeth. It is likely Thomas Seymour suffered some sort of breakdown at this time, for his behaviour became ever more bizarre. Disgruntled at being ousted from court prominence by his more successful older brother, Lord Protector, Edward Seymour, Thomas continued to dice with death. Determined to secure an audience with the young King Edward, he broke into his bedchamber, disturbing the boy's pet dog, who took umbrage at the intrusion. Thomas, probably in panic, shot the dog dead. For this, and for conspiring to marry the king's sister without consent, he was later executed. It was now impossible for Elizabeth to avoid further scandal.

Elizabeth's household were taken to the Tower for questioning. Elizabeth, when subjected to interrogation, denied any knowledge of a proposed marriage, or of an affair. Her servant, Thomas Parry, however, told his tormentors all they wished to hear. Ashley then had no option but to concur. When Sir Robert Tyrwhit rode in triumph to confront Elizabeth with these confessions, she refused to concede anything more than having refused to have anything to do with Seymour's proposal. This is the first indication we have of Elizabeth's enormous strength of character.

There is no first-hand account of Elizabeth's private feelings on the matter, she kept them to herself, but it seems she learned her lesson and from that time, she presented an outwardly modest appearance. For the first time, we glimpse the public mask that Elizabeth presented for the remainder of her life.

After the scandal broke and she first appeared in public, she chose a simple gown, unadorned and much plainer than the other court women, utilising clothing as a screen from public scrutiny. From this time on, it took all her wit to survive what must have been miserable and dangerous years until she became queen in 1559. Once queen, she threw off her assumed modesty and embraced the elaborate style of dress now associated with her.

As queen of a male-dominated country, Elizabeth refused to marry and instead, as if to belie the rumours about her and Seymour, embraced the ideal of purity, and chastity. Her agenda was to convince her subjects that she was more than a woman; she was her father's daughter and as capable as he.

The message of the powerful Virgin Queen was stressed in the portraits throughout her reign. Elizabeth embraced magnificence; each emblem and outfit bore a coded message, even the colour of the stones she wore had significance. There are few descriptions of the queen's appearance early in her reign because those who met her seem to have been hard pushed to see beyond her finery, but as her rule progressed, and her magnificence increased, there are written descriptions as well as the famous paintings with which to compare them.

As a young woman, she favoured black and white, describing them as 'her colours'. Black represented wisdom and stability and, by happy chance, also provided the perfect backdrop for her beloved jewellery. White symbolised purity and red was for power, yellow for fruitfulness and green for youth. In the early part of her reign, when her looks were still full of vitality, the queen's wardrobe enhanced her beauty and flattered her lithe upright figure, but as she aged, she used the majesty of her clothing to obscure her physical decline. Elizabeth, the Virgin Queen, was ageless.

Under Elizabeth, the female form entirely altered. The upper body was elongated and narrowed to a point, and about the waist, a French farthingale resembled a cartwheel. The fabric of the skirt spread out horizontally from the waist, like a tabletop, before cascading to the ground. This style, together with huge puff sleeves, created the iconic Elizabethan outline. As discussed previously, during Elizabeth's rule, the modest ruff of the previous reign became huge. Despite this extraordinary style and reshaping of the feminine form, Elizabeth does not seem to have been extravagant when it comes to money spent on her wardrobe.

The Coronation Portrait is housed in the National Portrait Gallery and was painted around 1600; it is a copy of a lost original. It shows the queen in a gown of cloth of gold which had previously been worn by her sister Mary, at her own coronation. She holds the orb and sceptre, and her hair is loose, to emphasise her virginity. In this painting, her ruff is of modest size, and she is not wearing the cartwheel farthingale, but her expression is glazed, her feelings masked.

The Ditchley Portrait, also housed at the National Portrait Gallery, illustrates the more extravagant style for which she is famous. She wears a white gown which is bejewelled with ouches and worn over a French farthingale. Her sheer ruff is lace edged and appears to be attached to her partlet or the straps of her bodice. The shape of her body is completely obscured. She is neither male nor female for in this painting she has become something more, she has become a goddess.

The Rainbow Portrait (see Plate 11) is kept at Elizabeth's former home, Hatfield House, in Hertfordshire. It was painted quite late in her reign, yet she appears not a day older than in images that were painted much earlier. Embroidered on her dress are ears and eyes, a curious choice when viewed from the twenty-first century, but they served as a subtle, symbolic reminder to her subjects that she was fully aware of everything that went on in her kingdom – even the smallest plots and conspiracies.

The flowers embroidered on her gown are also symbolic; the lily for purity, the rosemary, as Ophelia in Shakespeare's *Hamlet* reminds us, for remembrance, and of course, the Tudor rose, the emblem of her house. The queen is wise and cunning, something summed up by the snake on her sleeve. Her wealth and majesty are displayed by the rich fabrics and her costly jewels – the pearls illustrate her virginity and the crown, of course, is symbolic of her rule.

Plate 3: Anne Boleyn, *The Hever Portrait*, English school. (*Public domain, Wikimedia Commons*)

Plate 4: Jane Seymour by Hans Holbein the Younger. (*Public domain, Wikimedia Commons*)

Plate 5: Anne of Cleves by Hans Holbein the Younger. (*Public domain, Wikimedia Commons*)

Plate 6: Uncertain identification, could be either Katherine Howard or Anne of Cleves, by Hans Holbein the Younger. (*Public domain, Wikimedia Commons*)

KATHARINE PARRE.

Plate 7: Katherine Parr, unknown painter, National Portrait Gallery. (*Public domain, Wikimedia Commons*)

Plate 8: Edward VI attributed to William Scrots, active 1537–1553. (*Public domain, Wikimedia Commons*)

ANNO DNI · 1 5 4 4 ·

LADI MARI DOVGHTER TO
THE MOST VERTVOVS PRINCE
KING HENRI THE EIGHT

THE AGE OF XXVIII YERES

Plate 9: Mary I by Master John, National Portrait Gallery. (*Public domain, Wikimedia Commons*)

Plate 10: Young Elizabeth I by William Scrots, Royal Collection. (*Public domain, Wikimedia Commons*)

Plate 11: Elizabeth I, *The Rainbow Portrait*, attributed to Isaac Oliver. (*Public domain, Wikimedia Commons*)

Plate 12: Elizabeth I, *The Ermine Portrait*, attributed to William Segar. (*Public domain, Wikimedia Commons*)

Plate 13: Elizabeth I in coronation robes, National Portrait Gallery. (*Public domain, Wikimedia Commons*)

Plate 14: Queen Elizabeth I, *The Ditchley Portrait*, by Marcus Gheeraerts the Younger. (*Public domain, Wikimedia Commons*)

Plate 15: Henry Howard, Earl of Surrey, attributed to William Scrots. (*Public domain, Wikimedia Commons*)

Plate 16: Thomas Howard, 3rd Duke of Norfolk, by Hans Holbein the Younger. (*Public domain, Wikimedia Commons*)

Plate 17: *Portrait of a Standing Boy*, attributed to Wybrand de Geest. (*Public domain, Wikimedia Commons*)

Plate 18: Portrait of Catherine Hooft and her nurse by Frans Hals. (*Public domain, Wikimedia Commons*)

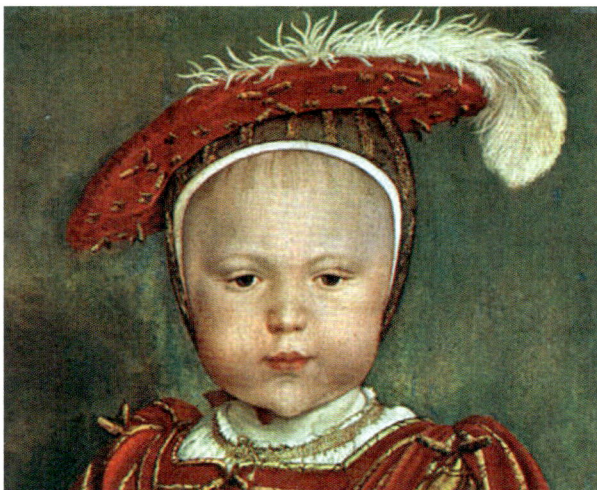

Plate 19: Infant Edward VI by Hans Holbein the Younger. (*Public domain, Wikimedia Commons*)

Plate 20: Count Fortunato Martinengo Cesaresco by Moretto da Brescia. (*Public domain, Wikimedia Commons*)

Plate 21: Catharina van Warmondt by Isaac Claesz van Swanenburg 1596. (*Wikimedia Commons*)

Plate 22: Henry VIII and his fool from the Psalter of Henry VIII. (*Wikimedia Commons*)

Plate 23: Cardinal Wolsey, Christ Church. (*Public domain, Wikimedia Commons*)

Plate 24: Henry VIII's wives, circle of R. Burchett Parliamentary Art Collection. (*Public domain, Wikimedia Commons*)

Plate 25: Thomas Culpepper and Katherine Howard. (*Photograph: Judith Arnopp*)

Plate 26: The Fyne Companye of Cambria and Friends. (*Photograph: Lorna Mclean*)

Plate 27: The author as a Tudor goodwyf. (*Photograph: J. Arnopp*)

Plate 28: The author in her French gown. (*Photograph: J. Arnopp*)

Plate 29: A cheerful Henry VIII. (*Photograph: Judith Arnopp*)

Plate 30: *The Field of The Cloth of Gold*, unknown author. (*Public domain, Wikimedia Commons*)

Plate 31: The king and crew. (*Photograph: Judith Arnopp*)

Plate 32: The author's family. (*Photograph: J. Arnopp*)

Plate 33: The Duke of Norfolk at Laugharne Castle. (*Photograph: Judith Arnopp*)

Plate 34: Minstrel Tom of Raglan Castle. (*Photograph: Jane Mcilquham*)

Plate 35: Henry VIII and Anne of Cleves at Aberglasney. (*Photograph: Glynis Riddle*)

Plate 36: Duke of Norfolk and Mary Tudor at Laugharne Castle. (*Photograph: J. Arnopp*)

Plate 37: The author playing a grumpy Queen Mary I at Laugharne Castle. (*Photograph: J. Arnopp*)

Plate 38: The Fyne Companye of Cambria at Laugharne Castle. (*Photograph: Lorna Mclean*)

Plate 39: What is this sorcery?
(*Photograph: J. Arnopp*)

Plate 40: The Fyne Companye of Cambria on a hot day at Aberglasney Gardens. (*Photograph: Jeff Taylor*)

Plate 41: Lady Judith and Lady Morag. (*Photograph: Lisa Lucas LRPS*)

Figure 36: Elizabeth I, *Ditchley Portrait*, by Marcus Gheeraerts the Younger. (*Wikimedia Commons*)

You may think at first glance that she is clutching a length of Perspex pipe, but it is the shadow of what once represented a rainbow, the paint now sadly worn away. But in its day, when the paint was vibrant and fresh, Elizabeth held in her hand the biblical symbol of peace. Some of her other portraits include the sun, which was the symbol of monarchy, but in this painting, there is no need for it. The inscription 'non sine sole iris' translates to 'without the sun, there can be no rainbow' and since the queen has the rainbow in her grasp, it must therefore mean that Elizabeth stands as a metaphor for sun or, in other words, only Elizabeth can create peace.

More than any other Tudor monarch, Elizabeth understood and made full use of the power of clothing, but surprisingly she was relatively frugal (some might say tight-fisted) when it came to expenditure. As mentioned earlier, for her coronation, she repurposed a gown worn by Mary at her coronation in 1553 and many of her later gowns were remade, the fabric salvaged, and some gowns were altered to fit, or restyled. At her death, there were reports that she owned 6,000 gowns, but Eleri Lynn thinks it more likely that she owned the modest number of 'two thousand items, including separate parts'.[15] To look as good as Elizabeth did on a relatively tight royal budget is skilful indeed, but her frugality owed more to necessity than natural thriftiness.

When she became queen, she inherited a virtually bankrupt country, and she did all she could to ease the debt, including limits on her own personal expenditure. The Master of her Great Wardrobe, Sir John Fortescue remarked, 'As for her own private expenses, they have been little in building; she has consumed little or nothing in her pleasures. As for her apparel, it is royal and princely beseeming her calling, but not sumptuous or excessive.'[16]

Eleri Lynn points out that in the last four years of her reign, Elizabeth spent roughly £9,500 on her wardrobe, yet in the first five years of her successor, James I, the king spent an eye-watering £36,000 *per year*.

Chapter Five

Shirts – Styles and Use

Shifts and shirts

As I have mentioned in previous chapters, a garment of linen was worn next to the skin by both sexes, children and adults alike. Since the shift was intended to be frequently washed, it was invariably made of linen; the higher on the social scale the wearer, the finer the quality of the fabric. Even among the upper classes, the outer clothing was never laundered due to the fabric from which it was constructed. Even today, garments of that kind would be sent out for specialist cleaning, but the Tudors had to make do with brushing their best clothes. Linen, however, not only stands up well to regular laundering and can withstand scrubbing but it softens and improves with wear.

The man's base layer, referred to variously as a 'shirt' or 'shift', was a simple geometric shaped garment that remained largely unchanged throughout the period. Made of a series of rectangles and squares with a triangular gusset beneath the arms, they were easily made. Men's shirts were designed long, with deep slits on either side to allow the back 'tail' to be brought up between the legs, to cover their nether region.

The higher one's status, the finer and whiter the grade of one's linen. For lower classes, the shirt was unadorned and made from coarse linen, fastening at the neck and sleeve with ties. Of course, when it came to the nobility, the parts of the shirt that would be most prominently on display, the front, neck, and sleeves, were heavily embroidered with black or red work, sometimes with additional seed pearls.

Although the basic shape remained the same throughout the period, as time went on, variations were made to the neckline and collar in keeping with the changing style of the outer layers. Early Tudor examples illustrate a simple upstanding collar, which around 1535 began to develop into a small gathered or ruffled neck. By the 1550s, Mary Tudor was painted wearing a small but multiple-layered ruff; a style which by the 1570s had expanded in height to around four inches. The contrasting embroidered edge, which was fashionable in earlier examples, was replaced by lace edging and the ruff became detachable – this evolution into a separate garment was presumably for ease of laundering. Similar changes occurred in the male garment.

The discovery of starch facilitated the ruff to be made larger and larger, the soft folds formed into an extravagant figure of eight shape with the use of a heated 'goffering iron'. The larger style of ruff was impractical both to wear and launder, which made them suitable only for the very wealthy, but it didn't prevent aspiring classes from aping the style. During the Elizabethan era, at the height of the ruff's popularity, an estimated ten yards of fabric was required for just one ruff and a pair of cuffs.

I'd always imagined ruffs only came in white, but apparently other colours were available. During her disputes with Scotland, Elizabeth I banned the wearing of blue-dyed ruffs because it was the colour of Scotland's flag.

Initially ruffs were worn tight to the neck but later were attached to the neckline of a kirtle or gown, leaving the throat exposed. This new fashion didn't find favour in all quarters. Social critic Stubbes condemned the style quite harshly.

The women there [in Ailgna] use great ruffes, and neckerchiefs of holland, lawn, cambric, and such cloth, as the greatest thread shall not be so big as the least hair that is: then, least they should fall down, they are smeared and starched in the devils liquor, I mean Starch: after that, dried with great diligence, streaked, patted and rubbed very nicely, and so applied to their goodly necks, and, withall, underpropped with supportasses (as I told you before) the stately arches of pride: beyond all this they have a further fetch, nothing inferior to the rest; as, namely, three or four degrees of minor ruffes, placed gradatim, step by step, one beneath the other, and all under the Maister devil ruff. The skirts, then, of these great ruffs are long and wide every way, pleated and crested full curiously, God wot. Then, last of all, they are either clogged with gold, silver, or silk lace of stately price, wrought all over with needle work, speckled and sparkled here and there with the sun, the moon, the stars, and many other antiquities strange to behold. Some are wrought with open work down to the midst of the ruff and further, some with purled lace so cloyd, and other geegaws so pestered, as the ruffe is the least part of itself. Sometimes they are pinned up to their ears, sometimes they are suffered to hang over their shoulders, like windmill sails fluttering in the wind; and thus every one pleases herself with her foolish devices, for suus cuiusque crepitus sibi bene olet, as the proverb saith: 'everyone thinketh his own ways best'.[1]

Stubbes was a social critic, whose book, *Anatomie of Abuses*, concerned the vices taking place on the 'mythical' Isle of Ailgna. This was a not very subtle anagram of Anglia, which once served as an alternative name for England. It is an amusing if sometimes startling read that provides otherwise unobtainable information about the Elizabethan society he condemned. His descriptions are in the tone of an outraged twenty-first century grandparent seeing his granddaughter's ripped jeans for the first time, but that doesn't make his observations any less honest. Elizabethan fashion was extreme, uncomfortable, and not far short of ridiculous, so I tend to agree with Stubbes.

The largest, most extreme style of ruff was known as the 'millstone' and was up to a foot wide, requiring wire or pasteboard supports to keep it straight and upright. While the smaller styles were attractive, the larger ones were bewilderingly impractical, suitable only for the elite.

In England, the wearing of ruffs had largely gone out of fashion by the early seventeenth century, but continued to be worn longer in the Dutch republic. Even today, ruffs continue to have a small place in our world, worn not only by re-enactors but also by some clergy and, of course, choir boys.

Doublets

We have all seen television dramas in which the men are strutting around in just a doublet and hose. It looks dead sexy to us, but the Tudors would have been appalled; doublets were never worn as an outer garment, shirts would have been even more shocking. To appear in public, and most especially attend court, without a coat would have been like going to the pub without your trousers. Eyebrows would most definitely be raised.

Before the Tudor period, doublets were often plain and serviceable rather than decorative, their main object was to hold up the hose, which was fastened to the doublet by points. They ended at the waist, with a short two-inch skirt to conceal the lacing. They were usually long-sleeved and fastened down the front with further points. Over this, in the medieval period, it was the fashion to wear a houppelande gown. This was a long full-skirted garment worn by both sexes, belted at the waist, and often had wide, sweeping sleeves. Later in the era, the man's version became shorter, evolving into a loose gown that one could wear open at the front to reveal the doublet beneath.

In the years that followed, the doublet became more visible and much grander, embellished with surface embroidery and gems, and the sleeves were often puffed and slashed as fashion dictated. The front waistband shifted from the natural waist to form a point lower down, the small 'skirt' evolving into a peplum that was made up of several tabs. Attachments known as 'wings' were introduced on the shoulder to disguise the ties for long sleeves. The front of the doublet was padded, and later this padding was increased to create what came to be known as 'bombast', providing a shape known as the peascod belly. This fashion fad was quite opposite to today's requirement for well-toned abdominal muscles. As far as the Tudors were concerned, a man who could eat well enough to grow a paunch was rich, and therefore powerful – a fact that was worthy of celebrating. In 1583, a book was published by Philip Stubbs in which he provided many hilarious if rather harsh criticisms of the current fashions.

> For what may these great bellies signifie else than that either they are such, or els are affected that way? ... For certain I am there was never any kinde of apparell ever invented that could more disproportion the body of man than these Dublets with great bellies, hanging down beneath their Pudenda (as I have said), & stuffed with foure, five or six pound of Bombast at the least. I say nothing of what their Dublets be made, some of Saten, Taffatie, silk, Grograine, Chamlet, gold, silver, & what not; slashed, jagged, cut, carved, pincked and laced with all kinde of costly lace of divers and sundry colours, for if I should stand upon these particularities, rather time then matter would be wanting.

Stubbs seems to have been the earliest fashion critic – you should see what he says about the women!

By the seventeenth century, the tradition of hiding 'points' was dispensed with, and it became fashionable to fasten the top and bottom clothing together with large floppy bows. The fashion for doublets died out with the introduction of long coats with waistcoats beneath, worn with full breeches, as favoured by King Charles I.

Chapter Six

Codpieces and More

The codpiece must be the most talked about aspect of male Tudor clothing. My husband remarked after his first ever outing sporting a fine purple velvet 'piece' that he'd never had so many people look at his crotch in his life. So, the codpiece clearly works very well as an advertising tool (if you'll excuse the pun).

In the early Tudor period, men's legs were encased in hose, a two-piece garment rather like stockings, which were attached by points or laces to the doublet via eyelets at the waist. This left the area between covered only by the tucked under shirt (see previous chapter). This gap had previously been concealed by a long tunic and mantle but as fashion changed and doublets grew shorter, a greater degree of covering became necessary. This gap in the buttock area was already posing problems before the Tudors came to the throne. Henry VIII's grandfather Edward IV's parliament made it compulsory for the 'privy Members and Buttokes' to be covered. Geoffrey Chaucer illustrates the problems shorter doublets caused in *The Canterbury Tales*, in which the parson decries the ridiculous fashions of the day.

> On the other hand, to speak of the horrible inordinate scantiness of clothing, let us notice these short-cut smocks or jackets, which, because of their shortness, cover not the shameful members of man, to the wicked calling of them to attention. Alas! Some of them show the very boss of their penis and the horrible pushed-out testicles that look like the malady of hernia in the wrapping of their hose; and the buttocks of such persons look like the hinder parts of a she-ape in the full of the moon.

Clearly, if this was not just the overactive imagination of an author, something needed to be done. Early codpieces were relatively discreet additions to the male attire, comprising of a triangular flap of fabric,

Figure 37: Henry's codpiece, detail from portrait by Hans Holbein the Younger. (*Wikimedia Commons*)

attached by points, and this style remained in common use among the peasantry throughout the period. This provided not only modesty but also a convenient 'pocket' to keep one's valuables which later gave rise to the slang term 'the family jewels'. Perhaps it was this manner of storage that instigated rivalry between gentlemen as to who wore the biggest 'piece', for by the middle of the sixteenth century, the size of the codpiece had swollen to such a degree that it drew the eye from the other finery and became a symbol, not of size or wealth, but of fertility.

Ironically, despite his desperate quest for a son, Henry VIII is famous for sporting the largest codpiece of them all. It is impossible to view his portraits, or indeed his armour, without the attention being drawn to his splendid piece. The one pictured above equals the splendour of his other clothes; it is slashed, and silk lined, embroidered, and constructed in such a way as to stand proud from his skirted kirtle. In Henry's case, it was all part of the royal propaganda, a loud statement, *I am the King of England, and I will get a son… just as soon as I find myself a fertile wife*. In Henry's eyes, his failure to produce an heir was, of course, always the fault of his wives.

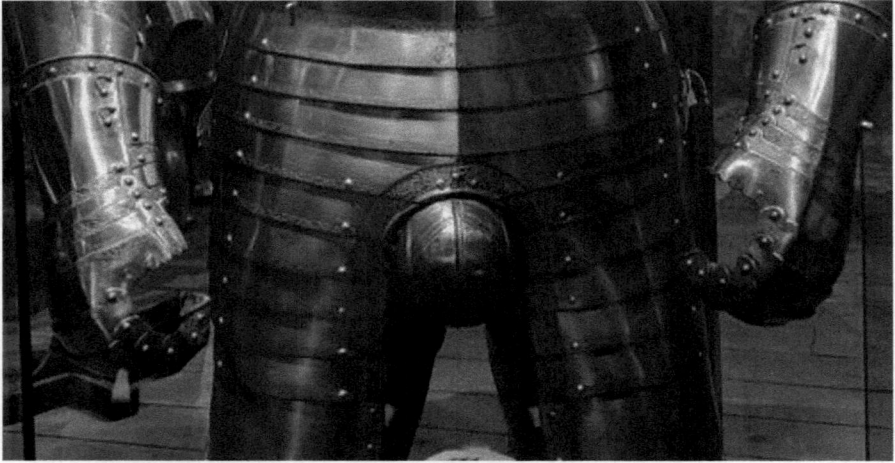

Figure 38: Henry VIII's armour codpiece. (*Photograph: Simon Arnopp*)

Gentlemen, not just in England but all over Europe, followed suit. No matter how unremarkable the male member beneath, the codpiece that concealed it was a proclamation of lusty manhood. They were brocaded, bejewelled, embroidered, tasselled, and beribboned. Even prepubescent boys were obliged to adopt the fashion as Plate 8, a portrait of Edward Tudor, illustrates.

At court, the codpiece was a mark of virility, of manhood, and a promise of future heirs. On the battlefield, it signalled ferocity. In the centuries that followed, female visitors to the Tower of London, where Henry's codpiece was on display, would stick pins in the inner lining in the hopes of increasing their chances of conception. I can only hope it brought them more success than it did Henry.

By the late 1500s, the popularity of the codpiece had declined with the changing shape of the male outline, when the traditional doublet shape was replaced by the peascod or goose belly. This was an extraordinary look. As discussed earlier, the torso of the doublet was padded, and sometimes boned. The waist at the back and sides remained in the natural place but the front was cut lower, which, together with padded trunk hose, concealed the genitalia to focus on the exaggerated outline of the torso. The favour of this false fat belly seems strange to the modern world where we do all we can to appear thinner, but in the Tudor era, a good belly denoted wealth, which everyone aspired to.

ANNO DOMINI · 1568 ·
ÆTATIS   SVÆ · 4 4 ·

Figure 39: Thomas Wentworth, 2nd Baron Wentworth, sporting a fine peascod belly doublet, formerly attributed to Hans Eworth. (*Wikimedia Commons*)

Chapter Seven

Headwear

In the Tudor era, the headwear of the upper classes was more to do with status than keeping one's ears warm. The quality of the fabric and the construction of the hat said as much about one's station in life as one's outer clothes. A man's cap could inform as to his job of work. Black was a more difficult dye to achieve and therefore a more expensive shade, worn only by those who could afford it. Remnants of red and blue caps, hues much easier to achieve, have been preserved in river mud, suggesting they were colours favoured by the lower classes, perhaps those who worked on the river or the dock.

Most caps were knitted and then felted to make them waterproof, and most were round and sported either a part or full brim. Usually, a coif was worn beneath the cap, as illustrated in the portrait of the Duke of Norfolk but the coif was also used by those of the professional class, as shown in the painting by Holbein the Younger of Henry VIII and the Barber Surgeons.

Figure 40: Henry VIII Parliament Procession Roll 1512. (*Wikimedia Commons*)

Sailors wore what was known as a Monmouth cap, a round knitted hat rather like the beanie that is popular today.

Reputedly the only surviving item of Henry VIII's wardrobe is his Cap of Maintenance, which is housed at the Waterford Museum. The hat and bearing sword were gifted by Henry to the mayor of Waterford in 1536. The cap is made from Italian velvet and the crown is stiffened by baleen, a substance that comes from a whale, used to filter plankton from the sea. This is believed to be the earliest surviving use of baleen in clothing.

The outer is embroidered with a Tudor rose, with daisies stitched around the brim. The rose to symbolise the Tudor dynasty and the daisies (Marguerites) as a nod to his grandmother, Marguerite Beaufort. The Cap of Maintenance was carried aloft on a pole before the king on his coronation procession.[1]

Everyone in the Tudor era wore a hat of some kind. It was not acceptable to appear in public without one. Legislation even decreed where one's cap should be made. As early as 1488, the Cappers' Act forbade the wearing of foreign made caps in England and Wales. The act was amended in 1571, during the reign of Elizabeth I, ordering that everyone above the age of six, excluding 'Maids, ladies, gentlewomen, noble personages, and every Lord, knight and gentleman of twenty marks land' must on Sundays and holidays wear 'a cap of wool, thicked and dressed in England, made within this realm, and only dressed and finished by some of the trade of cappers, upon pain to forfeit for every day of not wearing 3s. 4d.'[2]

Like many acts of the period, this proved a difficult law to govern and was repealed again in 1597.

The flat cap was often referred to as a 'bonnet' and was a style favoured by Henry VIII and his son Edward VI. It is a style we immediately associate with King Henry, but this type of hat was worn by every stratum of society. Commoners wore a knitted and felted version but those favoured by the upper classes were made of far finer fabrics, such as felted wool covered with silk. The nobility and royals wore the best fabrics of all, their caps being usually made of velvet and heavily embellished with pearls. There are some surviving examples of beaver caps, and the more expensive styles were lined with silk, the interior as exquisite as the outer. But it seems that flat caps were not exclusive to men; Figure 41 is a portrait of Katherine Parr wearing a fine feathered version over a shaped and pearled coif.

Figure 41: Katherine Parr wearing a masculine-style hat, unidentified painter. (*Wikimedia Commons*)

Another style was the four-cornered cap, which was worn from as early as 1480 and appears to have been favoured by the likes of clergymen, mayors, and physicians. The four-cornered style came in several versions: some had extensions that could be pulled down to cover the ears, which was especially useful in draughty, unheated buildings, or the flaps could be tied up on top of the head. Other examples had no extension at all.

Figure 42: Sir John Hawkins by Hieronimo Custodis. (*Wikimedia Commons*)

Yet again, we have Holbein to thank for providing details of this style of headwear. His sketch of Thomas More (Figure 8 – see Introduction) shows him wearing a four-cornered cap with perhaps a black coif beneath.

After the 1560s, the crown of the hat grew taller until it eventually evolved into the high-crowned style we are accustomed to seeing on Guy

Fawkes from the Jacobean era. The style quickly became popular, and women adopted it too, together with a high-necked, masculine-style bodice and ruff.

This new masculine style of dress led to criticism in some quarters, giving voice to fears that women were encroaching on the male domain. The portrait of Admiral Sir John Hawkins (1532–1595) shows what appears to be pleating on the crown and a hat band embellished with jewels, and a fine jewelled hat pin.

Most hats of this type were constructed by pulling fur or wool felt over a block form to create the tall crown and flat brim. They were made of wool or velvet but, although far more expensive, another more luxurious option was felted beaver fur.

Chapter Eight

Men's Gowns and Coats

In the late medieval period, the difference between basic male and female clothing was less pronounced than in the Tudor era. Both sexes wore a houppelande (sometimes referred to as Burgundian gown). It was a loose garment, belted at the waist or beneath the bust, with wide sleeves – a voluminous garment that provided warmth and ease of movement. For those high up in the social scale, the houppelande was richly lined and trimmed with fur or velvet.

During the early part of Henry VII's reign, the court continued to be influenced by this French and Burgundian style. The upper echelons at court, who were able to afford the quantity of expensive fabric required, wore them not only to keep warm but to advertise their status and wealth. The houppelande could be ankle or calf length and was usually dark in colour, black being a difficult hue to achieve and therefore more desirable. In the early years of the Tudor reign, clothing was largely undecorated and even fur was used sparingly until Henry VII was replaced by his more flamboyant son.

As the Tudor era progressed, this style of gown was replaced in the gentleman's wardrobe by a shorter, box-shaped garment, opening at the front to reveal the sumptuous doublet and jerkin/kirtle beneath. Henry VIII's love of ostentation was quickly adopted by his courtiers, the new look reflecting the style of the new vibrant monarch and the onset of the Renaissance period. The shorter demi-gowns showed off more leg at a time when a man's shapely leg was as of much interest as a well-toned torso is today.

Henry was immensely proud of his well-defined calf muscles, on one occasion quizzing his courtiers as to his legs being far shapelier than those of his rival, the French king, Francis. At this stage, Henry was still handsome and physically fit, showing tremendous prowess at hunting, jousting, tilting, and tennis. Giustinian, the Venetian Ambassador to the

English court, described him as 'the handsomest potentate I ever set eyes on: above the usual height with an extremely fine calf to his leg…'

Henry loved sport, and was seemingly tireless, often wearing out his courtiers in his early years as king. He was also a trendsetter. During a game of tennis in 1527, Henry injured his foot, probably resulting in a bad sprain, and during recovery took to wearing a single black velvet slipper, which led to his courtiers adopting the fashion.

Although a courtier was expected to reflect the glory of the king, he took care to never rival him, and it is clear from court portraiture that, on the whole, they were careful not to outdo him. On occasion, though, it seems one of two of them went a little too far.

Edward Stafford, the Duke of Buckingham, overstepped the mark on several occasions, the first being during Henry VII's reign at the wedding of Arthur Tudor and Catherine of Aragon. In 1513, he attended a meeting between Henry and Maximillian wearing a gown of purple satin, embellished with antelopes and swans, worked in gold with spangles and little bells. Buckingham was of Plantagenet extraction, a family that Henry treated warily due to the threat they posed to the Tudor line. Tudor monarchs had little love for those of Plantagenet blood, especially those who flaunted it and, although no action was taken straight away, his paper was marked. He was arrested in 1521 for plotting to replace Henry VIII on the throne.

> In Gilbert's evidence the Duke was accused of purchasing cloths of gold and silver, to the amount of 300 marks, for the purpose of distributing them in presents to the King's guards; of endeavouring to obtain a licence from the King for arming certain of his subjects in Wales;—a charge not unlikely to be true, and, considering the disorders of the principality, and the Duke's large possessions there, not necessarily indicative of any felonious intention.[1]

Another nobleman who overstepped the mark was Henry Howard, the Earl of Surrey, who not only irritated the king with his ostentatious clothing but dared to remind people of his royal blood. The ageing Henry VIII became paranoid that after his death, Surrey planned to usurp the throne from his heir, Edward. When Surrey went as far as to quarter the attributed arms of Edward the Confessor, thus proclaiming his right to the throne, the king took the opportunity to imprison both Surrey and his father, the Duke of Norfolk, in the Tower of London. Surrey was executed just prior to King Henry's death in January 1547, but his father, Norfolk, escaped punishment at this time. He remained in the Tower throughout Edward's reign until his old enemy, Mary, inherited the crown. Mary, putting a fellow Catholic before personal resentment, released Norfolk in 1553 (see Plate 16).

There are few examples of prosecutions under the sumptuary laws, so we can only assume they were ineffective. The very fact that the laws were constantly amended suggests that the legislation was largely ignored but changing fashion also necessitated a change in the directive. The few records we do have of offences seem petty to modern eyes, used as we are to seeing all sorts of fashion faux pas.

In 1565, Richard Walweyn found himself in trouble for wearing 'a very monsterous and outraygous greate payre of hose'. It is frustrating that the account does not go into more descriptive detail. How I would love to see an illustration of those 'monsterous' hose. His offence could have been due to the Elizabethan fad of padding the calf muscle to give the illusion of a shapelier leg, or it could have simply been a case of using more fabric than his status allowed. He was a member of the servant class and, as such, only permitted a yard and three-quarters to stuff his stockings.

Further investigation illustrates how the lower classes have always tried to ape their betters. In 1576, a Fellow of King's College was imprisoned for wearing 'a cut taffeta doublet and a great pair of galligastion hose' beneath his gown. Galligastion hose were baggy, again requiring more fabric than a simpler cut. It is unclear how long the poor fellow remained in jail, but breaking these laws could lead to the loss of livelihood, and not just the temporary loss of liberty.

An attorney by the name of Kinge went before the Privy Council 'in apparel unfit for his calling, with a guilt rapier, extreme greate ruffes and lyke unseemelie apparel' and as a result, he was dismissed from his job.[2]

The legislation of 1553/4 remained unchanged until the acts were repealed in 1604 after the accession of King James. During her time as queen, Elizabeth made twelve proclamations amending the laws, doubling the number of changes made by her father, Henry VIII. To her credit, most of Elizabeth's reasons were not to preserve her status as a fashion icon but attempts to benefit the country. Most of her prohibitions were placed on imported goods, thus strengthening, or attempting to strengthen, English industry. This continued into the next reign when in 1662 imports of 'foreign bonelace, cutwork, embroidery, fringe, bandstrings, buttons and needlework'[3] were prohibited.

Henry VIII's iconic outline is recognisable the world over and it owed much to his demi-gown; the massive shoulders of which were wired and padded, richly decorated, and trimmed with cloth of gold. An inventory of Henry VIII's wardrobe from early in his reign suggests he owned an astounding 128 gowns in twenty-seven different fabrics. Henry's wardrobe was housed at the Tower of London, and it is estimated that the king spent £8,000 a year on clothes, which equates to something around £2,500,000 today. Alison Weir, in her book, *Henry VIII: King and Court*, states:

> In 1517, James Worsley, the Keeper of the Royal Wardrobe in the Tower of London, listed some of the items of Henry's clothing in his care, including 'mantles, gowns of cloth of gold and velvet, coats, jackets and doublets, glaudkyns (surcoats), bases, girdles, belts, furs and sables, powdered ermines, cloths of gold of divers colours, velvets, satins, damasks, sarcanets and linen cloths.'[4]

When it came to Henry's clothes, the lining was of equal importance to the outer fabric. He owned a purple tinsel mantle lined with lambswool, a green velvet gown lined with green satin, and a surcoat made from white cloth of silver and lined with cloth of gold. When one considers the forty-one gowns, twenty-five doublets, twenty-five pairs of hose, twenty surcoats, sixteen frocks – meaning loose surcoats – seven jerkins, ten cassocks, eight cloaks, fifteen Spanish capes, twenty-three girdles and sword belts, purses, bonnets, shirts, gloves, slops and so on that he owned in the year 1547, it is a wonder he ever managed to decide what to wear.

The true value of such an enormous wardrobe is not apparent until one considers the costs of the fabrics used in such quantities. The most expensive fabric was silk or its derivatives, like brocade, satin, and velvet. Cloth woven with gold and silver was more expensive still. Purple velvet cost around 41s 8d (£625) a yard. Weir puts cloth of gold at a cost of £2,170 a yard. Multiply these costs with the number of garments Henry had stashed away at the Tower and you come to quite a hefty sum.

Lace didn't become fashionable at court until Catherine de Medici introduced the Italian method of lace making in France. It spread from there into England, where Catherine of Aragon founded a cottage industry of lace making and embroidery in the Fens in the 1530s and women began to experiment with Spanish blackwork and cutwork.[5]

Ecclesiastical clothing had long been adorned with embroidery, but it was not until the early sixteenth century that it became popular in lay clothing. Black silk embroidered headdresses, collars, and cuffs were introduced to England via Spain and the Low Countries. Whereas ecclesiastical embroidery had once been worked by nuns, after 1515, the embellishment of upper-class clothing was produced by the Worshipful Company of Broderers.

Although Catherine of Aragon was not responsible for introducing blackwork as so many historians in the past have claimed, she was nevertheless a skilled needlewoman. Not only was she responsible for Henry's embroidered shirts, but also embellished altar cloths and church vestments. George Cavendish recorded in his book *The Life of Cardinal Wolsey*:

And then my lord rose up, and made him ready, taking his barge, and went straight to Bath Place to the other cardinal; and so went together unto Bridewell, directly to the queen's lodging: and they, being in her chamber of presence, showed to the gentleman usher that they came to speak with the queen's grace. The gentleman usher advertised the queen thereof incontinent. With that she came out of her privy chamber with a skein of white thread about her neck, into the chamber of presence, where the cardinals were giving of attendance upon her coming.[6]

Chapter Nine

Men's Accessories

Jewellery, sashes, and shoes

Jewellery has always been the domain of the rich, but nobody loved a bit of bling more than Henry VIII. Between 1529 and 1532, he spent £10,801 on jewellery alone. Not only for himself and his queen but also as gifts to friends and mistresses. Not that Henry was wasteful. Jewels were recycled wherever possible. He insisted the jewellery belonging to Queen Catherine of Aragon was passed to Anne, and so on and so on to subsequent queens. The same items of jewellery can be identified in a succession of royal portraits from the Henrician period and are believed to have been remodelled in the later reigns of Henry's heirs.

Every king needs a crown, but Henry didn't stop there. He wore a collar made of heavy gold, decorated with rubies and pearls that hung about his shoulders. His medallion, illustrated in several portraits, was set with four emeralds. He possessed more than one, some were chains of office, but others were merely for show. Chains of office are still in evidence today but until the dissolution, they were only worn by those of status. After the dissolution (c.1539), monastic gold was melted down and remade into chains and sold to wealthy merchants who wished to emulate their betters.

Henry, it seems, saw fit to embellish every garment. His underclothes were embroidered with cloth of gold, his slashed doublet and kirtle were decorated with pearls, his false sleeves were fastened with jewelled clasps. He wore huge rings on his fingers and even his hat was ringed about with pearls. An encounter with Henry would leave nobody in any doubt as to who he was. As with everything else, this ostentation trickled down through the court, but the nobility, although similarly clad, were nothing in comparison with their king.

Jewelled clasps were square or round cut stones, mounted on ornate gold; they had a pin beneath, rather like a modern-day brooch, and were used to fasten the lower edge of the sleeve. Depending on the extravagance and depth of one's sleeve, this usually required four or five clasps. They could also be sewn on, but the majority were pinned into place, and, for seemingly obvious reasons, they are often referred to as 'ouches'.

After the dissolution of Canterbury Cathedral, Henry acquired from their treasury a ruby and a diamond that he had made into rings. I like to think they are the rings he is wearing in the Castle Howard portrait, but there is no evidence for this. Some historians have claimed that the Tudors did not favour diamonds but there are references to them in the record. They are difficult to identify in Tudor portraiture because when the portraits were painted, the artists often used silver pigments to capture the lustre of the stones, and this pigment has tarnished over time, making the painted stone appear to be black.

Henry was fond of rings; an inventory from 1527 records seven: a ruby, an emerald, and a turquoise, a table diamond, a triangular diamond, and a 'rocky' diamond. Herbert Norris, in his book *Tudor Costume and Fashion*, explains a 'rocky' was 'a term usually applied to a species of ruby and sometimes to a diamond'.

Aglets have been used since the medieval period to decorate and prevent fraying at the end of laces, and continued to be used both as a means of fastening the clothing and to provide further embellishment. I have a particular fondness for aglets, and I use them whenever possible, decorating them further with tiny seed pearls. Today, aglets have faded from modern dress, only existing in the form of the roll of plastic at the end of our shoelaces. A sad, meagre shadow of their former glory.

Pendants are probably the most recognisable Tudor jewel. They are seen on almost every portrait from the period. Made of gold with jewelled settings, they were square, or diamond shaped, or in some instances, a cross. Catherine of Aragon wears a cross pendant in her 1526 portrait. It is hung on a light chain and decorated with emeralds, rubies, and pearls. It is believed to have contained a relic.

In Holbein's painting of Jane Seymour, she wears a ruby and emerald pendant with a single pearl suspended by a gold and pearl necklace, with matching billament on her gabled hood and bodice.

For the re-enactor, the starting place for affordable Tudor-style jewellery is Etsy, where many artists produce and sell replica jewels from Tudor portraits and TV shows.

If you compare the shape of the sole of a shoe worn around 1485, when the Tudor dynasty ascended to the throne, with one from the height of Henry VIII's reign, it will reveal a vast change in fashion.

The late medieval shoe for both sexes was narrow and pointed but still roughly foot shaped. As the period progressed, the style gradually grew shorter and wider but maintained a pointed toe. By the 1500s, the toe was broad, often fastened with a strap, rather like the Mary Jane shoes that are popular today. By Henry VIII's time, the broad-toed style of shoe was referred to as 'duck billed', the slashing on the upper making them resemble the claws of a lion. Many female re-enactors wear a modern Mary Jane shoe since they can be concealed beneath their voluminous skirts. For male re-enactors, the feet are more on show and, apart from armour and weaponry, footwear can be one of the costliest purchases they have to make.

By the sixteenth century, a new style of manufacture was introduced in which the upper shoe was attached to the insole and welt, a second row of stitches being made through the welt to attach to the sole, offering more flexibility and, presumably, comfort.

For outdoor wear, the sole was made of wood or leather, the upper of leather. Indoors, courtiers often wore slippers, a softer backless 'mule', presumably to mute the clatter of wooden soles on the palace floors. These low-backed styles required a higher front over the instep to prevent the wearer from walking out of them. The uppers were made of velvet, silk, or satin, or soft leather, often slashed, embroidered, and decorated with pearls, depending on one's status. Cork was used between the upper and the sole, and there is some evidence for footwear with a sole made entirely from cork.

Henry VIII's portraits from the latter half of his reign show him wearing low-backed, square-toed, slipper-style shoes in an off-white to match his hose. In one portrait, the 'cuttes' or slashes form the shape of a flower, above and below a line of decorative pearls. As is commonplace with fashion, Henry's style was adopted by courtiers and those wishing to emulate their superiors. The popularity of broad-toed shoes grew so extreme that in the end, the king issued a sumptuary law to prohibit excessive breadth.

Of course, these impractical styles were not adopted by everyone – most people's purse would not allow them to compete, and men of business, apprentices, or lawyers stuck to more sober, substantial shoes.

For riding and hunting, long boots were worn. Although never to the extremes of the court shoe, the toe did become squarer toward the middle of the period. The boots reached the mid-thigh and were made of best-quality substantial leather and usually dyed black, brown, or tan. Prospective re-enactors please note that long leather hunting boots were never worn at court as you so often see depicted in television historical drama and film.

Dressing like a fool

It doesn't matter how far back you research into history, if there is a monarch present, then his fool will not be far away. In one form or another, be it tumbler, juggler, trickster, jester, or clown, every recorded culture had them, but, thanks to Shakespeare and other writers of the period, it is the motley fool of the English medieval kings that remains uppermost in our minds. But these fools were not simply to amuse the monarch, they had other, more subtle duties and their importance shouldn't be underestimated. As the sixteenth-century author Erasmus pointed out: 'We have all seen how an appropriate and well-timed joke can sometimes influence even grim tyrants ... The most violent tyrants put up with their clowns and fools, though these often made them the butt of open insults.'[1]

There are many historical mentions of court fools. Dwarves, of course, and warrior fools, Norman buffoons, minstrel fools, and innocents, but it is the Tudor fool, Will Somer, the fool and close companion of Henry VIII, who is the best documented.

Somer was not the only fool at the royal court, but he seems to have been the king's favourite. His predecessor, Sexton (also sometimes known as Patch), was a natural fool, a person with special needs who was gifted to the king by Thomas Wolsey. He was famous for his nonsensical wit but did not wear 'motley' uniform to mark him as a fool; instead he was given top-quality clothing, with a carer to ensure his needs were met, and his food and lodgings were also provided. Natural fools were valued members of the court, believed to be closer to God and therefore nurtured.

The historical record suggests Will Somer was less a wit than a natural fool. Today we would refer to this as having learning difficulties, but the thing that set him apart from the others was the king's regard. He had the ability to turn Henry's mind from problems when it needed turning the

Figure 43: Engraving of Will Somer, the king's fool. (*Wikimedia Commons*)

most. The most famous quip afforded to Somer is by Thomas Wilson, who quotes him in *Art of Rhetoric* as follows.

> William Somer, seeing much ado for account-making, and that the King's Majesty of most worthy memory, Henry the eighth, wanted money such as was due unto him: As please your grace (quoth he) you have so many fraud-iters, so many conveyers, and so many deceivers to get up your money, that they get all to themselves...

The pun on 'auditors, surveyors and receivers' is both a joke and a truth, and there are other similar witticisms recorded to Somer in other works of the period. For example: Armin's *Foole upon Foole* (1600), Samuel Rowley's *When You See Me, You Know Me* (1605), or the anonymous *A Pleasant History of the Life and Death of Will Summers* (1676).

John Southworth, author of *Fools and Jesters at the English Court*, says that these documents do not offer much in the way of history, but they all highlight Somer's use of his 'merry prate' and spontaneous rhymes to improve his master's state of mind.

William Somer first emerges in the historical record of 1535 when an order appears for new clothes for 'William Somer, oure foole'. This was around the time when Henry's 'olde foole' Patch/Sexton had grown too old, and Will was chosen to take his place.

His initial requirements included a fool's livery:

> a dubblette of wursteed, lined with canvas and coton ... a coote and a cappe of grene clothe, fringed with red crule, and lined with fryse ... a dublette of fustian, lyned with cotton and canvas ... a coote of grene clothe, with a hood of the same, fringed with white crule lyned with fryse and bokerham.

Throughout his service, Somer was maintained by the privy purse, for although there is a surviving record from Cromwell in January 1538 of a 'velvet purse for W. Somer', there is no mention of anything to fill it, his expenses presumably being met by the court.

In this fine new apparel, Will Somer's sole duty was to entertain and distract the king from his worldly care, and he seems to have done so admirably. His favour with Henry raised him so high that he even makes an appearance in several portraits, commissioned by the king himself. The most famous is the family portrait by an unknown artist which is now housed in the Royal Collection.

It is what might be termed a fantasy painting that depicts Henry at his most virile and vigorous best, and Queen Jane, who at the time of painting had already been dead for over a decade. On the king's right is their son, a prepubescent Edward Tudor, whose birth caused his mother's death in 1537. Completing the Tudor idyll are the princesses, Mary and Elizabeth, both girls bastardised and legitimised so many times that they can have had no real idea as to their royal standing.

The entire royal family are assembled in a fictional gathering, a made-up truth to please the king, and what makes this especially poignant is that a little behind the royal sitters, the painting also shows Will Somer, dressed in his 'clothe coote' with his green velvet purse hanging from his belt. His pet monkey is obligingly picking lice from the fool's hair.

Framed in the opposite archway is a likeness of a girl, believed to be Jane, the innocent fool who belonged to Princess Mary. It is believed Jane may once have 'belonged' to Anne Boleyn but was taken into Mary's household after the queen's execution. The presence of the royal fools in this very personal portrayal of Henry's family can only point to their importance. They were not simply court members but part of the family.

Another glimpse we have of Will Somer is in a psalter commissioned by Henry in or around 1540. This time, the king is portrayed as an old man, in the character of King David. He presents a lonely character, sitting alone in a chamber playing a Welsh harp, with only his fool for company. Will is pictured with his back to the king. Again, he is dressed in the 'grene cloth cote' recognisable from the descriptions in the privy purse accounts.

Since most of Henry's old friends had by this point been executed, exiled, or, more rarely, died from natural causes, there must have been few left whom he could safely trust or confide in. This makes the image of the lonely old king and his trusty fool hauntingly sad.

Records suggest that, as the king aged and his health deteriorated, only Will was able to take Henry's mind from the incessant pain of his ulcerated leg, the continual cares of state, and his ever-increasing ill-health and depression. Right until the end of the king's life, wherever

Henry went, Will went too; from palace to palace, his every need catered and provided for.

At Christmas 1545, just a year before the king's death, when a batch of sixteen horses were ferried across the Thames on a trip to Hampton Court, there were three mounts to carry the massively obese king, and one for his fool, 'Wyllyam Somer'.

After Henry's death in 1547, Somer went on to serve at the court of Edward VI and Mary I, but he fades from the record and died early in the reign of Elizabeth. He is buried at St Leonard's in Shoreditch, his name marked on a stone to commemorate players and musicians of the period who are buried in the church.

Ecclesiastical clothing

There isn't room in this book to provide more than a brief outline of ecclesiastical clothing. Up until the closure of the monasteries, the religious community in the sixteenth century was vast, with its own social structure. A similar set of rules was applied throughout, affecting all members of the religious community, be they monks and nuns or bishops and archbishops, cardinals, and not forgetting, of course, Henry's friend, the Pope. For the duration of this chapter, I will be focusing on the Cistercian monks, with whom I am more familiar, but other orders were available.

By the period in question, monasticism had moved a long way from the Rule of St Benedict, a set of guidelines concentrating on frugality and humility, the focus of a monk's life being prayer and work. The rule was written around 516 and intended as a guide for monastic communities living beneath the authority of an abbot. The guidelines are harsh, the prescribed life arduous and comfortless, the only reward presumably being found in God's approval. When it came to clothing, St Benedict was specific and stated that clothing should be no more than adequate and

suited to the climate and locality, at the discretion of the abbot. It must be as plain and cheap as is consistent with due economy. Each monk is to have a change of clothes to allow for washing, and when travelling is to have clothes of better quality. Old clothes are to be given to the poor.[2]

He went on to allow that in winter a woollen cowl could be worn and in summer a lighter weight one. Sandals and shoes should be worn, suitable to the climate. He ordered that monks should not complain about the colour or quality of their garments and that when garments were replaced, the old should be distributed to the poor. Two of each garment should be provided to allow for laundering and repair – anything more was superfluous.

The monastic house had a communal wardrobe from which brothers embarking on a journey were provided with a better garment than that worn within the monastery for work. Underwear was also available for travelling monks but must be washed and given back on their return. This is interesting in that it suggests underwear was worn at this early date, although not necessarily every day or by everyone.

From this small example from the rule, we can see simplicity was key, and presumably at the time of writing (516), St Benedict was already concerned by sliding monastic practices and intended his rule as a tool to bring them back into line.

In 1068, things having declined further, a group of disillusioned monks, led by Robert of Molesme, broke away from their main Benedictine community and formed their own group known as the Cistercians.

The order spread across Europe and throughout England and Wales. The first Cistercian foundation in England was at Waverley, founded in 1128. There were originally just twelve brothers and an abbot, but by 1178, this number had increased to fifty monks and 120 lay brothers. Seeking peace and time to pray, they established their foundations 'far from the concourse of men' and for a while they embraced austerity, applying it to their way of life, their monastic buildings, and their clothing.

Orderic Vitalis, an English-born monk writing around 1135, noted that the Cistercians were distinguished by their use of undyed garments in contrast to the usual black – it was this that led them to become knowns as the White Monks. We should remember that black dye was difficult to achieve and therefore costly. The description of Cistercian clothing as 'white' doesn't mean the snowy white we are familiar with today but refers to unbleached wool, so would have been a natural off-white colour.

A monk's clothing consisted of under clothes, named variously as drawers and braies. Cistercians famously wore none at all. There was an ongoing dispute on whether or not monks should wear drawers. In his rule, Benedict had not stipulated 'drawers' as a requirement but it should be remembered he lived and wrote in the Mediterranean, where the climate made this desirable. For monks living and working farther north, it was impractical, and by the sixteenth century, most monks wore them. The Cistercians, however, keen to adhere strictly to the Rule of St Benedict, chose to go without. They claimed the cold air helped contain any impious impulse to sin. This made them the butt (no pun intended) of jokes.

During the reign of Henry II, the king and a group of priests were riding down a street when a Cistercian monk, hurrying to get out of the way, tripped and fell, exposing his bare bottom to the king.

The lord king, Henry II, of late was riding as usual at the head of all the great concourse of his knights and clerks, talking with Dom Reric, a distinguished monk and an honourable man. There was a high wind; and lo! A white monk was making his way on foot along the street and looked around, and made haste to get out of the way. He dashed his foot against a stone and … fell in front of the feet of the king's horse, and the wind blew his habit right over his neck so that the poor man was candidly exposed to the unwilling eyes of the lord king and Reric. The king, that treasure-house of all politeness, feigned to see nothing, but Reric said sotto voce, 'A curse on this bare-bottom piety'. I heard the remark and was pained that a holy thing was laughed at, though the wind had only intruded where it was rightfully at home. However, if spare diet and rough clothing and hard work cannot tame them, and they must have ventilation too to keep Venus at bay, let them go without their breeches and feel the draught. I know that our flesh – worldly and not heavenly though it be – does not need such defences: with us Venus, apart from Ceres and Baccus, is cold: but perhaps the Enemy attacks those more fiercely whom he knows to be more stoutly fenced in. Still, the monk who tumbled down would have got up again with more dignity had he had his breeches on.[3]

But I digress. Other orders did opt to wear drawers and also linen hose and a tunic which was often white with long close-fitting sleeves. Over this came a cowl or habit.

This was an ankle-length garment, with either short sleeves or sleeveless. Early in the period, the side seams were not sewn closed, but the habit was tied close to the body. The garment was hooded and served as everyday wear. As time progressed, the term 'cowl' came to denote a hood worn separately from the robe.

A frock was another ankle-length hooded item of clothing, worn for occasions or outside the monastery.

A scapular was a rectangular cloth, with a hole for the head to pass through. This garment was belted, it reached the ankles in front and back, and was worn over the cowl or habit with the hood pulled through.

A cloak was worn when travelling, usually made of woollen cloth in shades of black, grey, or brown.

Footwear was provided, closed or open, lined or unlined depending on the climate and the season. Slippers were also provided.

Early on, their economic success was likely to have been unlooked for. The founding fathers probably had every intention of adhering to St Benedict's Rule, but humility is not always easy. Through donations from benefactors, they came to possess huge acres of pasture, forest, and arable land and they worked hard clearing areas for further cultivation. They established granges (farms) that produced arable crops and were also involved with pottery production, iron mining and of course, sheep. As historian Janet Burton states in her article 'The Cistercians and Trade', 'They were not the first monastic farmers but they turned it into an artform.'[4]

I have mentioned the wool market in previous chapters; the Cistercians were key players in this trade and it added greatly to their rapidly increasing wealth. As time progressed, and their coffers grew fuller, their original intent was lost. Rules were broken.

The medieval period was a time of war, a time of crusade. When men went off to fight the infidel, fearing they would die in sin, they paid monks to pray for them; when they returned (if they returned), they made further donations to the church to compensate for the transgressions they had perpetrated overseas. Monies were paid for prayers for the dead. The monasteries grew rich, and since they were human, the abbots and bishops became greedy, and this was reflected in the style of buildings. Their humble churches of the early years built in the austere Norman style became more opulent. Forbidden embellishments in stone began to appear alongside stained-glass windows, decorative tiles, and splendid altars began to increase in number. All these things were forbidden in the rule which made the Cistercian establishments no less austere than their Benedictine cousins. Stories emerged of fat abbots feasting, drinking, and gambling, abbesses with fine silk petticoats, and pet dogs, living in luxurious apartments while the neglected brethren in their charge turned to sin.

By the sixteenth century, accusations of immorality increased. Whether these reports were wholly true continues to be a matter of debate. King Henry was at odds with the Pope, and soon to make himself Head of the Church in England. At the same time, Lutheranism was spreading across Europe and others were pressing for church reform, so it is difficult to judge the level of exaggeration in some of the stories. Either way, the days of monastic influence were numbered and in 1536, an act was passed ordering the suppression of monasteries valued at less than £200 per annum. Pensions were given to those who opted to leave the religious life, others were transferred to larger religious houses.

One by one, the abbeys began to fall, and those who protested were dealt with violently. The Pilgrimage of Grace, an uprising in the north, ultimately ended in many deaths and a great deal of suffering. Without the abbeys, the poor were left with no charity, no hospitals, no employment, and the roads of England began to fill with dispossessed monks and nuns, who lacked the ability or the will to seek new employment. By 1540, all religious houses had been closed, the inhabitants dispersed, and the lands and property rented or sold to those in favour with the king, or Thomas Cromwell.

So, in a roundabout way, I have established that the lowly monk was dressed rather more humbly than the average peasant. Farther up the scale, however, it was a different matter. Cardinal Thomas Wolsey, for example, was at the top of the tree in England. He showed little humility, either in dress or action. Born around 1473, the son of Robert Wolsey of Ipswich and Joan Daundy, his father traditionally described as a butcher, Thomas Wolsey was an ambitious man, driven by the need for power rather than faith, and he deported himself as extravagantly as King Henry VIII.

George Cavendish's book about Thomas Wolsey, written around 1554–1558, illustrates just how lavish his lifestyle was. On being made a cardinal, Wolsey sent to Rome for:

two or three hoods of such pattern and colour as Cardinals be want to wear there, and also one paper caps larger and shallower than those were which your lordship lately sent to me; with two great pieces of silk used by Cardinals there for making the kirtles and other like garments.

He preferred fine scarlet, crimson satin, taffeta, damask, and wore a tippet of sable about his neck and didn't shy away from cloth of gold; materials also favoured by the king and the royal family. Of course, cardinals and all bishops were expected to maintain a certain status, but Wolsey took it to extremes. Like many of Henry VIII's 'friends' who disagreed with his divorce from Catherine of Aragon, Wolsey made a sorry end, but he is a rarely seen yet worthy addition to any Tudor troop.

Clerical clothing was made up of cassock, surplice, rochet, and vestments (worn only by the clergy). The quality of the garments depended on the material and embellishments used to reflect the wearer's status and their place within the church.

Nicholas West, for instance, Bishop of Ely, who died in 1533, owned a kirtle of violet cloth furred with foin (fur of the marten), and two riding kirtles of camlet (usually mohair or angora wool woven from camel or goat) and say (worsted).

We have looked briefly at the lowliest and the highest of churchman in England. For the re-enactor, a monk often seems an easy option and it is simple and cheap enough to take on the persona of a Friar Tuck-type character in rough habit and sandals, but beware, there are just as many details to take on board before deciding the order and the status of the person you wish to recreate. There are a few basic monastic patterns available; a search of the internet will produce second-hand sellers of historical costumes and it is always worth checking eBay. I haven't yet made one, although I do know someone who would make a great cardinal, but he has yet to be persuaded. Examine portraits of your chosen figure, trawl through second-hand shops for likely scraps of brocade or woollen blankets (depending on your project), and you may be inspired.

It should be easy enough to up the status of a habit from monk to bishop just by using more opulent materials. The costs of enough woollen fabric and linen to make a reasonably authentic monk costume could be equal to creating a Thomas Wolsey from your mother's front room red velvet curtains. As always, it is advisable to ensure your costume, and the status of your chosen character, is obtainable within your budget. In my opinion, it is preferable to produce an authentic lower-class ecclesiastic than an obviously inauthentic cardinal or bishop.

Chapter Ten

Children's Clothing

Thankfully, the twenty-first century concept and expectations of childhood are vastly different to those of the Tudor era. Children were, of course, important, but in earlier centuries the emphasis was less about nurture and love, and more about their usefulness. A son, as he grew, would assist his parents, help boost the family business, increase productivity and income. Daughters would help their mothers about the house, assist with childcare, and when they married, their spouse's income, status, or family connections would be an asset to the family. Upper classes, too, valued their children, especially sons, to perpetuate the blood line, consolidate the family wealth, and a good match brought a dowry and sometimes property. When it came to kings, sons were vital for maintaining the dynasty. Daughters, although less desirable than sons, were useful ambassadors to be married to foreign kings to cement political alliances or peace treaties. While most children were treasured and loved, their importance to parental ambition cannot be ignored.

Some historians have argued that childhood didn't exist until the Victorian ideal of innocence became popular, and a study of Tudor portraits with children dressed in stiff unaccommodating clothing, posed in uncompromisingly adult attitudes, certainly seems to uphold that idea.

There were three stages of childhood: the first was infancy, the second from toddlerhood to the age of seven when boys were breeched, and the third from seven to fourteen when a child passed into adulthood.

Small children were dressed almost identically to their parents, although boys wore dresses modelled on their mother's until they were breeched at around the age of six or seven – this may have had something to do with the necessities of toilet training. Negotiating a small wriggling infant in long skirts would be hard enough, but fiddling with a codpiece and hose would have been even more difficult.

The Tudor era was lax when it came to toilet habits; grown men urinated in the street, and even gentlemen used the corridors of the royal court when nature demanded; children did the same. Since the lower classes spent much of their time outdoors where the light was better, infant 'accidents' in the lower echelons would not have caused a problem. Indoors, where rustic dirt floors were the norm, it wouldn't have mattered much either. When it came to bedtime, even in middling circles, I cannot imagine sheets were changed daily, whether they were wet or not.

A newborn infant was swaddled, tightly wrapped in the belief that this would ensure the limbs grew straight. This practice is often regarded today as rather cruel, but the Tudors believed it to be in the best interest of their child. The term 'swaddling' comes from the Dutch word to 'nourish and keep warm',[1] which suggests our opinion of the practice requires revision. It should be remembered that the Tudors lacked access to the safety equipment we take for granted, there were no stair gates or fire guards, no play pens, or highchairs to protect against falls, crushing, or other accidents. Infant bones are delicate – a broken bone in that era could easily become infected and quickly lead to death. It was also a great deal colder in the sixteenth century.

The Midwives Book: Or the Whole Art of Midwifry Discovered was published in 1671 by Jane Sharp, who had worked as a midwife for over thirty years. In it she advises women on conception, pregnancy, childbirth, and childcare.[2] When it comes to swaddling, she advises:

In the swaddling of it be sure that all parts be bound up in their due place and order gently, without any crookedness, or rugged folding; Infants are tender twigs and as you use them, so they will grow straight or crooked.

The Bridgeman art gallery holds a portrait of Cornelia Burch, aged two months, painted in 1581 by an unknown artist. There is no further information on Cornelia or whether she survived infancy, but she was clearly from a prosperous family. Her fine linen cap, gold rattle, and fancy cradle all point to her being from an important line. I always imagined swaddling bands were made of plain linen, but Cornelia's are silk and bound with gold braid. It is interesting to note that her arms are left free, but whether this was commonplace or not is open for debate.

There are other portraits illustrating fully swaddled infants, and I confess none of them look very happy (see Figure 44). The swaddling of very young babies included many layers. A rectangular cloth napkin with a layer of absorbent sphagnum moss. A belly binder to protect the belly button. Then came a linen shirt. The infant would have a triangular cloth and a cap. It was then placed into a sort of nest which was wrapped around and folded up over the feet. Then came the long swaddleband, which was wrapped around in a herringbone pattern. A bib was also worn

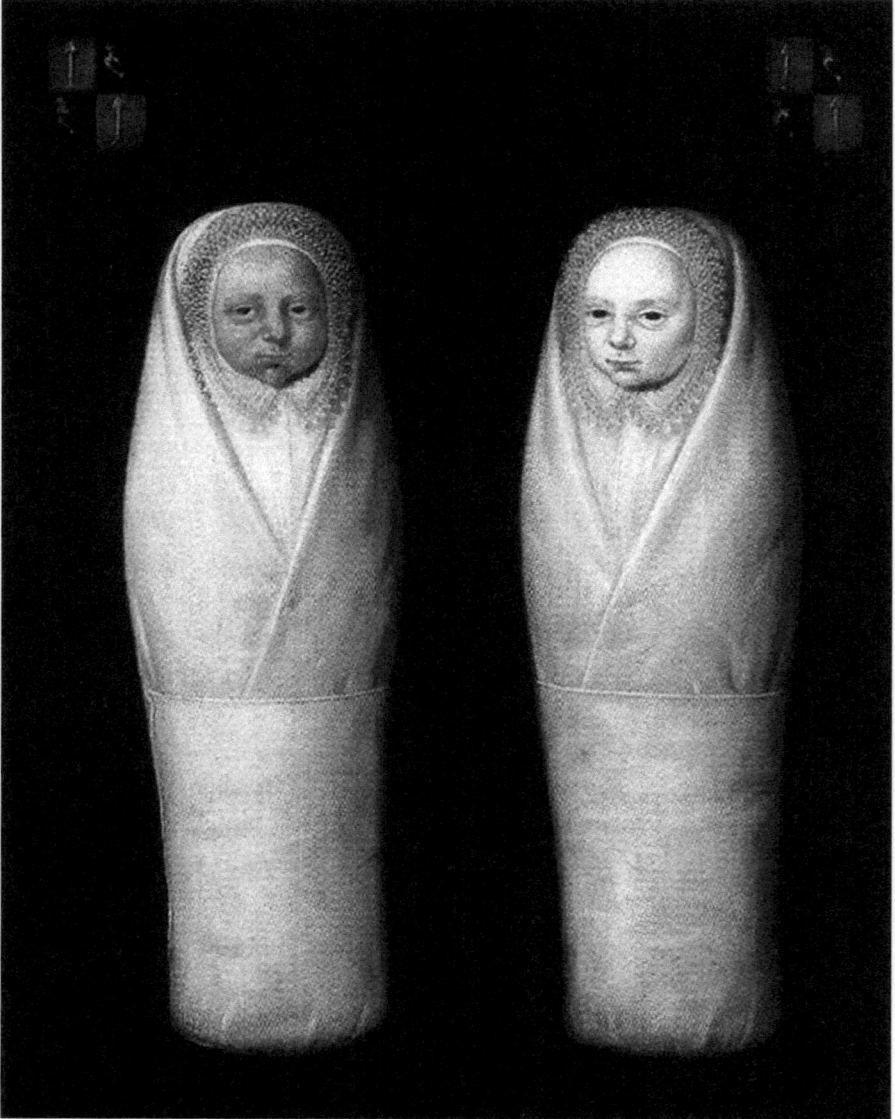

Figure 44: Swaddled twins, Rijksmuseum. (*Wikimedia Commons*)

and a 'stayband' to keep the head stable. This wrapping and dressing must have taken quite a while, yet the practice continued until well into the eighteenth century, when questions began to be raised on the safety of the practice.

In 1748, William Cadogan published an 'Essay upon nursing: and the management of children from their birth to three years of age', in which he observed:

> The Mother who has only a few Rags to cover her Child loofely, and little more than her own Breaft to feed it, fees it healthy and ftrong, and very foon able to fhift for itfelf; while the puny Infect, the Heir and Hope of a rich Family lies langufhing under a Load of Finery, that overpowers his Limbs, abhorring and rejecting the Dainties he is crammed with, till he dies a Victim to the miftaken Care and Tendernefs of his fond Mother.[3]

Cadogan and the research of John Locke, who wrote in 1693 *Some Thoughts Concerning Education*, were key in identifying the link between swaddled babies and infant mortality. By the end of the eighteenth century, in Britain at least, the practice of swaddling had been abandoned.

There is no concrete proof that I could find to suggest babies were kept permanently swaddled and they must have been unwrapped several times a day to have their linen changed. I like to think they were tightly wrapped when put down to sleep – warm, secure, and hopefully comfortable, but given adequate time to play and kick. I may, however, be overly optimistic.

Contemporary paintings and drawings illustrate toddlers of all classes wearing long skirts. Lower-class children wore identical clothing to the parents, coarse practical garments to facilitate their lifestyle. There was little if any schooling within lower-class families, mostly because it was believed to serve little purpose, but, from an early age, children of both sexes would have learned how to live. They would have been expected to perform 'chores' – scaring birds in the fields, collecting firewood, running errands, and girls as young as seven were regarded as reliable enough to mind their younger siblings.

There were standards of behaviour for all classes. Children were expected to respect adults and honour their parents. It was customary for upper-class children to spend most of the day with their nurse or governess and it was only in the evening that they spent a brief period of time with their parents, where they would kneel to receive a blessing. Echoes of this custom can be seen today in the form of the bedtime kiss.

Toys were simple, often homemade replicas of adult tools, cooking pots, plates, dolls, hoops, and hobbyhorses. *The Tudor Child* refers rather alarmingly to 'toy guns capable of firing a small charge'.

By their early teens, children were regarded as capable of adult work; some lower-class adolescents were apprenticed, some went into service. The children of noble class, both male and female, were customarily sent away from home to be raised in the household of a nobleman, where the boys would be taught swordsmanship alongside the usual Latin. Anne Boleyn spent her youth at the French court serving Queen Claude, the spouse of François I, and his sister, Marguerite of Valois. There she learned the fine necessities of courtly life and presumably learned them so well that on her return to England, her distinguished French manners attracted the attention of King Henry VIII himself – whether in retrospect that was a good or bad thing is a matter for debate.

Among the nobility, education began at a very tender age. By the age of four, Princess Mary had learned to play the virginals so well that she impressed the Imperial ambassadors. She was also fluent in Latin by the age of nine. Her sister, Elizabeth Tudor, also displayed a degree of talent for Latin translation that would be remarkable in a child today.

The rod was often the tool that spurred the child on but, of course, although at various times dismissed as illegitimate, Mary and Elizabeth were royal princesses, and the threat of physical punishment would not have been used as an incentive to study. However, their cousin, Jane Grey, later to become the ill-fated nine-day queen, was not so fortunate. By all accounts, she was as precociously intelligent as her royal cousins, yet she complained to the English scholar, Roger Ascham, of being

> so sharply taunted, so cruelly threatened, yea presently sometimes with pinches, nips and bobs and other ways (which I will not name for the honour I bear them) so without measure misordered that I think myself in hell.

The historical record provides few female voices and those of children are almost silent. Jane's complaints sound like a living hell but, just as everything else in history, the reliability of her account should be

Figure 45: Robert Pytts and his grandson. Circle of Robert Peake the Elder. (*Wikimedia Commons*)

questioned. It may indeed suggest she was the victim of abuse, or it could merely be the tantrum of a wronged teenager. When you consider the role her parents played during her fated nine days as Queen of England, their ambitions for Jane are clear.

It does seem that, compared to today, the educational expectations placed upon royal children were considerable. The expectation of good behaviour was similar across all classes. A Tudor child was expected to do as they were told, they were always expected to be subservient and polite, their desires of far less importance than that of their parents. This seems very different when viewed from the perspective of the twenty-first century, where, in many cases, the youngest generation has come to rule the household.

Contemporary portraits reveal very little about the day-to-day life of a Tudor child. They seem like little wooden statues, bereft of character, their voices silent, a momentary glimpse of them on their best behaviour. I very much doubt they were the little angels they appear to be, dressed in their finest clothes, clean, cute, and compliant. The portraits represent a side of them their parents wished to be seen, with the same intention as the carefully posed portraits of the adults. Offspring were an asset to be displayed with as much pride as a fine horse, or a newly built manor house.

To Henry VIII and his heirs, portraits were a display of status, of wealth and power. There are no paintings of Henry in his nightshirt or covered in sweat after an energetic game of tennis, yet we know he enjoyed sport and, like everyone else, went to bed wearing a nightshirt. Clearly, it would have been impractical and uncomfortable to wear such splendid clothing every day, especially in regard to the children. The court paintings should not be taken as evidence of everyday dress, and neither should we imagine that Tudor children spent much time at all in their finest clothes. I would imagine, once the portrait artist was done for the day, the children were swiftly divested of their finery and sent back to the nursery.

Infants

As mentioned earlier, infants were swaddled until around the age of eight or nine months, although there are a few accounts of an earlier 'escape'. After that, they were 'coated' in short coats or petticoats, both sexes wearing similar garments. Although almost identical, the boys' garment was referred to as a 'coat', while the girls' was known as a 'gown'. Boys wore 'petticoats' beneath their 'coats', while some girls wore 'kirtles'. It was only the name of the garment that differed; the function was the same.

A kirtle sewn for the two-year-old Mary Tudor in 1498 was made up of three yards of black satin, the skirts lined with black cloth, the upper

Figure 46: Catharina van Warmondt, Isaac Claesz van Swanenburg c.1596. (*Wikimedia Commons*)

bodies with linen. That is a considerable amount of expensive fabric for such a small child. In this period, kirtles were sleeveless, with an attached skirt, but they were not usually so fine; the excessive volume of cloth in Mary's kirtle was testament to her status as a royal princess.

Bibbed aprons were also worn and, as usual with all Tudors, the head was covered by a biggin, coif, or cap.

A variety of shirt styles seem to have been favoured, again replicas of the adult garment. The boys wore them long with slits at the side, to tuck between the legs and over the loins, while the girls wore shorter, knee-length garments.

Biggins (or coifs) were made of linen. This was a close-fitting cap that tied beneath the chin, as worn by people of every status, and most portraits featuring young infants illustrate the importance of keeping a child's head covered. Even in the 1970s, infants were still wearing a similar 'bonnet', usually knitted, with ties beneath the chin. They kept the head warm, were difficult for the child to remove, and looked lovely. In some paintings, all that is visible of the coif is a white band beneath a cap, but it can safely be assumed that a biggin was worn. Depending on one's class, a headband, cloth, or outer cap was pinned to the biggin to keep it in place.

In 1516, ten-month-old Mary Tudor was provided with 3,000 pins, an alarming thought when you consider how much babies like to wriggle. It wasn't just caps that were pinned but foreparts, placards, and sleeves; if Tudor women were anything like me, they left a scattering of pins in their wake, and in the case of infants, it must have been worse.

Children's headwear, whether biggin, cap or hood, were replicas of the adult style. Royal children wore the best fabrics, velvet of black and crimson with fine silk veils. Of course, these were highly embellished for court days, costing huge sums and contrasting sharply with the cheaper, rougher linen known as 'hamborow' that the lower classes wore. There are also examples of royal and noble children wearing fur hats and, further down the social scale, knitted caps.

Just as with the caps, children's clothing closely followed the style of garments worn by adults. Wide skirts, many layers, and after 1539, in the portraits at least, hanging sleeves begin to appear among the children of the elite. These sleeves did not hang from the wrist but from the shoulder, with the heavily embellished undersleeve fitting closely to the length of the arm.

Bibs and aprons would, I imagine, have been essential. These were sometimes pinned at the neck which, in an era before the advent of the safety pin, was no doubt a prickly item to wear. *The Tudor Child* tells us this was known as a 'slavering clout' during the medieval period, and the word 'bib' did not appear until 1580. There is little pictorial evidence of it and very few historic garments exist, so we are reliant on inventories and orderbooks for reference. As the child moved from swaddling bands into coats, the bibs were replaced by aprons.

Aprons were made of linen or canvas, most were of white, blue, or brown, and fastened with ties or fixed to a waist band, similar to today. There is also some evidence for a combination of bib to protect the chest with a separate apron worn below the waist.

Another addition to the child's wardrobe was the 'muckinder', which was basically a cloth tied to the clothes for mopping up dribble and other nasties. There are several references in the historical record that mention it. In Peter Erondell's book of 1605 entitled *The French Garden*, there is a wonderful conversation between a lady and her child's nurse.

Now swaddle him again, but first put on his biggin, and his little band with an edge, where is his little petticoat? Give him his coat of changeable taffeta, and his satin sleeves. Where is his bib? Let him have his gathered apron with strings and hang a muckinder to it. You need not yet to give him his coral with the small golden chain ... give him some suck, I pray you take heed and wipe well the nipple of your dug before you put it in his mouth...[4]

This short excerpt provides a snippet of Elizabethan life that illustrates that although a child of the era was not cared for directly by the mother, at least some of them took a keen interest in his well-being.

The best visual representation of a muckinder I was able to access is a painting of the Countess of Hertford and her son (Figure 47). It was painted circa 1563. It clearly illustrates his muckinder hanging from his waist. It appears to be made from linen and is decorated with a fine blackwork edging.

This quote also mentions a 'coral'. This was a teething device, fashioned from coral, and fastened to the clothing or around the neck with a gold chain or, in some cases, a ribbon. It was sometimes referred to as a 'rattle'.

Shakespeare's Birthplace Trust has a fine example in its collection, but that one is made of bone and is a combination of teether and rattle. This particular example has metal bells attached; something that would present a clear safety hazard to modern parents. Mistress Page in Shakespeare's *The Merry Wives of Windsor* mentions such a rattle:

My little son and three or four more of their growth we'll dress like urchins, ouphes and fairies, green and white, with rounds of waxen tapers on their heads, and rattles in their hands.

The Tudor Child, in a study of portraits, notes that

just under a quarter of babies and 1% of toddlers in the images surveyed had either a combined rattle and teething piece, or a simple teething piece. They were almost exclusively elite and equally divided between boys and girls. However, coral was not limited to the elite. A coral tipped with silver was stolen from the house of an Essex yeoman in 1576.

Boys

At around the age of seven or eight, boys moved from the care of women into the world of men. This progression was marked by a change in the garments they wore. Presumably now reliable when it came to toilet matters, skirts were abandoned in favour of long coats and hose. This transition was known as 'breeching' and presented a milestone in a boy's life.

The style of hose differs as the era progresses. Early on, boys wore knitted hose, while adult men wore hose made of bias-cut woollen cloth. Later in the period, adult hose altered with the addition of upper hose with decoration that included slashing and padding. The elite boys followed this fashion, but the working class continued to wear the much simpler one-piece garment.

Slops were an early form of leg covering, a baggy knee-length style favoured by youths and occasionally worn by adults. This garment was gradually replaced by breeches, plain woollen for the lower class, while the upper classes favoured fine fabrics.

Over the course of the period we are covering here, the style of doublet for men altered considerably but for boys they remained simple. Early in the era, the doublet was collarless, with plain sleeves, and was front fastening. Toward the end of the era, the neckline became square and was worn lower, with some styles fastening at the side. The more fashionable (and affluent) child sported slashing – a form of decoration that involved slashing the upper fabric to allow the fine silk undergarment to peek through.

Toward the end of the reign of Henry VIII, the neckline evolved into the high standing collar and small wings on the shoulders, both to increase the apparent breadth and manliness of the shoulder and to also help conceal the points joining the sleeve to the body of the garment.

The shape of the doublet continued to evolve alongside that of the adults, and by the Elizabethan period, the waist was V-shaped at the front with tabs along the lower edge. Depending on class and status, they could be made of linen, wool, or silk or a combination of the three. The upper echelons were highly decorated with braid, sequins, and fancy buttons, while the lower classes wore simpler, more serviceable garments.

On top of this, until around 1560, a coat was worn. This garment was ankle-length and usually plain sleeved, although the wealthier and more fashion-conscious might have had puffed upper sleeves during the reign of Henry VIII. The coats grew shorter as the period progressed and were knee-length by the 1550s.

Figure 48: *Portrait of a Standing Boy*, attributed to Wybrand de Geest. (*Public domain, Wikimedia Commons*)

Gowns were worn by boys of the middling and upper classes – the elite favouring velvet with a fur lining to keep the chills at bay. Portraits of Edward Tudor, both as heir to the throne and king, illustrate the very pinnacle of a fashionable boy's gown with lavish goldwork embroidery and thick fur lining and collar. By the end of our period, for both men and boys, the vogue for gowns had fallen out of favour.

As gowns were discarded, cloaks became more evident among older boys, sometimes matching the coat worn beneath, sometimes contrasting with it.

The term 'girdle' evokes an image of women from the 1960s struggling into their Miss Mary of Sweden corset, but in the Tudor era, the term referred to a strap encircling the waist. We would probably call it a belt. The girdle could be fashioned from gold and jewels, or it could be made of fabric.

Noble women hung pomanders or prayer books from theirs, and housekeepers suspended the tools of their trade – keys. Men are depicted with daggers or short swords tucked or suspended from their girdles. In Holbein's famous painting of Henry VIII, he wears a silk girdle with an attached sheath and dagger. Scholars have been depicted with inkhorns and pen holders dangling from theirs. Before the 1600s, boys favoured girdles more than belts. They served to hold a child's muckinder, or perhaps a dagger or sword among elite older boys.

Girls

Unlike their brothers, girls remained in the care of women until they reached maturity. As they grew, they were taught the skills and tasks that would be required in later life. For the lower classes, this meant housewifery and childcare. Girls from higher echelons learned to manage a large household, social niceties, and, most importantly, the graces required to attract a good husband.

The very highest in the social scale were sent to other noble households, where they would perhaps have the opportunity to forge connections to serve them and their families. Anne Boleyn and her sister, Mary, spent time at the French court, where both acquired manners that enabled them to turn the head of Henry VIII when they returned to England.

Girls wore versions of adult fashion that changed subtly as they grew. It was a gradual process, unlike the milestone cut-off transition of 'breeching' their brothers enjoyed. Lower-class girls wore garments cut down from their mother or sisters' discarded clothing. Their clothes would have been economically cut and usually unembellished, although this may have been brightened up by the addition of ribbons if their pockets allowed.

Upper-class girls, of course, wore finer fabrics with plentiful embroidery, and their skirts and sleeves used a quantity of cloth. Portraits show sisters dressed alike but with subtle, age-appropriate variations; the rule of thumb seems to have been that the younger the child, the simpler the style, although still of best-quality brocades. Some portraits of female siblings suggest that although they wore clothes of identical fabric, the older sisters sported a more fashionable or grown-up style, with extra lace, embroidery, and fashionable extras like ruffs, fancy sleeves, and more extravagant headwear.

There is some confusion over the difference between a kirtle and a petticoat, and this is apparent both in the period and now. *The Tudor Tailor* explains the difference and presumably the same applied to children's petticoats:

A woman's outer clothes consisted of various combinations of petticoat, kirtle, gown, and jacket. Which of these she wore, and how many of them at one time, depended on her rank, the weather, the occasion, and the gradual evolution of fashion through the century … The garment worn by all women over the smock consisted of a fitted bodice with attached skirt. In the early Tudor period, this was called a kirtle. By the 1550s, the word 'petticoat' was being used to describe this item of clothing and 'kirtle' referred to a garment that was worn over, or instead of, a petticoat by wealthier, more fashionable women.[5]

The garments we shall refer to as 'petticoats' for the duration of this chapter were simple front-opening garments with pleated or gathered skirts. Some had a full bodice, some a scooped bodice with shoulder straps, some were just fastened around the waist like a skirt. It was common for the parts that would not be seen to be made from cheaper or more durable material, the visible parts more ostentatious. Red was a favourite colour throughout the period because the hue was believed to have properties that were health giving and warmer!

Kirtles that formed the third layer (after shift and petticoat) were made from more expensive fabric, especially the parts that would be seen: the forepart and the top edge and straps of the bodice. Worsted was favoured by the lower and middle classes, while satin was preferred by the rich. A kirtle for a six- or seven-year-old would require up to three and a half yards of top fabric. It would usually be lined with linen, and the hem trimmed with velvet. If the garment had sleeves, then more yardage would be used.

Sleeves were a separate garment that could be changed independently of the kirtle. They were attached at the shoulder with points. This allowed for new sleeves to be made as the child grew, or to be easily replaced if they became soiled. For the richer, more fashion-conscious girls, separate sleeves could be exchanged to provide a fresh look. It was common, when ordering the fabric for a new kirtle, to request enough for two pairs of sleeves to be made, to serve this purpose. As the era progressed, wider, boned sleeves and hanging sleeves became popular with older girls.

As with the adult women, a top gown was constructed from the finest fabric one could afford. A well-turned-out child was as much a symbol of parental status as a well-dressed wife. The portrait of Eleanor of Austria (see Figure 23) from around 1490 shows her wearing a square-necked gown with a black embroidered kirtle beneath; her sleeves are quite narrow and trimmed with ermine – in fact, it might be that her gown is entirely lined with fur. It is also interesting to note that her hood is clearly made up in three separate layers, as I discussed in Chapter Four about French hoods.

Later, the French gown gained popularity and remained fashionable until the end of the 1500s. This style of gown had wide outer sleeves, usually trimmed with fur or velvet, together with elaborate inner sleeves, which were slashed to show the silk lining. The sleeves were always fastened and embellished with jewels.

Holbein the Younger's sketch, *Woman on a Settle with Four Children*, illustrates that even the toddlers dressed in court clothes, while his more informal painting, *The Artist's Family*, shows an infant wearing just a shift and petticoat.

The gowns of young girls were not boned or heavily stiffened but interlined with canvas or occasionally strengthened with canvas on the

Figure 49: Woman on a Settle by Hans Holbein the Younger. (*Wikimedia Commons*)

inside lining. It wasn't until they reached adolescence that girls started to wear the extreme stiffened and boned bodices, presumably to support their developing breasts.

While the French gown was popular among the upper classes, working-class girls seem not to have worn them. Pictorial evidence points to a preference among poorer women for petticoats and waistcoats until the second half of the century and even suggests gowns were worn only by the daughters of gentlemen.

When looser English gowns were introduced later in the period, only older girls seem to have adopted them. These gowns were front opening, with a high neck and standing collar, and either long or short or puffed sleeves.

Another style, known as the Spanish gown, was of a more masculine cut, sporting for the first time a separate skirt and bodice, although there is some evidence that the bodice of the younger girls was attached to the skirts.

It was acceptable for small children and unmarried girls to have their hair uncovered but many portraits illustrate that headwear was worn. For the working classes, this was probably a matter of practicality as it is neither safe nor practical to perform manual tasks with long hair flowing around one's shoulders. Like their elders, working-class girls wore linen coifs, kerchiefs, or bonnets, while the upper classes, particularly in court circles, favoured elaborate styles based on the adult fashion.

Hair was seen as evidence of fertility, and long flowing hair was a matter of pride. In 1527, Henry VIII was still an affable, well-intentioned monarch who had every hope of securing his daughter and only heir, Mary, a lucrative foreign marriage. On St George's Day of that year, the king showed off Mary's talents to a company of ambassadors to the court. She was instructed to display her considerable grasp of languages, her skill as a musician, and her grace on the dance floor. As Henry had intended, the Venetian ambassador, Spinelli, was clearly impressed and wrote:

> They were all clad in tissue doublets, over which was a very long and ample gown of black satin, with hoods of the same material, and on their heads, caps of tawney velvet. They then took by the hand an equal number of ladies, dancing with great glee, and at the end of the dance unmasked; whereupon the Princess with her companions again descended, and came to the King, who in the presence of the French ambassadors took off her cap, and the net being displaced, a profusion of silver tresses as beautiful as ever seen on human head fell over her shoulders, forming a most agreeable sight. The French ambassadors went to see Mary at Greenwich. After dinner, Henry led them into a hall in which Mary, Katharine and the French queen were present, with a large company of ladies and gentlemen. The proud father told the ambassadors to speak to his daughter in Latin, French and Italian, and she was able to respond in all three languages. She also wrote in French for them, before performing on the spinet.[6]

Although hair was seen as a girl's 'crowning glory', it was also viewed by some with suspicion and thought to be indicative of promiscuity. At a wedding or other court appearances, it was customarily worn long and flowing; Anne Boleyn wore hers long at her coronation but otherwise kept it partially hidden beneath a cap. Married women kept their hair covered, as it was intended only for the delectation of their husband in the privacy of the marriage chamber.

As a rookie re-enactor, after struggling to keep my coif and hood in place on my shiny smooth conditioned hair, I've recently experimented with a Tudor hairstyle. The braided style really helps to keep the coif in place and secure the hood with ease. There are videos on YouTube that explain the method and it is surprisingly simple to do and stays in without the use of elastic bands or pins. It is remarkably comfortable, and you can even sleep in it, which is perfect for re-enactment weekends, when getting ready in the mornings is sometimes tricky.

First, you take a long length of linen ribbon and plait it into your hair by making two firm braids from just behind the ears. Then you flip each braid over the top of your head, well to the back of your crown. Then, using a stout bodkin, such as you might use for sewing with yarn, you sew the ends of the ribbon through the hair on your scalp. This style creates a Tudor ridge, which allows the ties of your coif to be fastened up and around the back and dispenses with the need to secure it beneath the chin. You may require the assistance of an obliging friend, but I have seen people do it themselves. The style is authentic and flattering. In fact, it sometimes seems a shame to cover it with a coif.

Chapter Eleven

How You Too Can Dress Like a Tudor

Before you start to sew your outfit, there are a few things you should consider. Do you know the basics of sewing? Straight seams, a few simple stitches like running, backstitch, and whipstitch are essential and easy to learn. Purists shun the use of a sewing machine but for the sake of speed and my failing eyesight, I often use the machine to sew long seams that won't be seen, but all my finishing, visible seams, and decoration are handsewn. This is not merely a matter of preference, though, because some groups will only accept clothing that has been entirely and authentically handsewn.

NB: Before making clothes for re-enactment, it is advisable to first check with the dress code requirements of your group.

The next thing to consider is where you intend your historical garments to be worn. Don't think for one moment that a 'not quite accurate costume' will be welcome at every re-enactment. Do check with your group's guidelines, they vary wildly.

Then think about the status of the character you'd like to re-enact. Lower-class costume is usually cheaper to put together than high-status clothing, the fabrics are easier to acquire, and they are also much more comfortable and cooler to wear. When I am trigged out as a Tudor queen, I am always too hot and often envy the lower classes, who seem to be having so much more fun. They usually have a trade, so this is something else you could consider before you begin to sew.

Research is key, not just for your clothing but for your proposed status or trade. There were a vast number of trades and places in society that can be represented: apprentices, cordwainers (leather work), weavers, tailors, smiths of all sorts, masons, carpenters, barbers, servants, merchants, prostitutes, sailors, paupers. Then there are the ecclesiastical members of society: monks, nuns, novices, bishops, priests, friars. I could go on.

Perhaps you already have a hobby that suggests an ideal slot for you to fill, something that would be easy to take along and set up on re-enactment days. A spinner perhaps, or a chandler, or maybe you are posh or have aspirations and would prefer to be a lady or gentleman.

You can pick a historical figure, do your research, and even base your costume on a portrait of your chosen character. If you choose to do this, you must get to know their history and be able to respond quickly and accurately to questions. The public are better informed than you might think. I've been told any number of inaccurate 'facts' by re-enactors who are unaware of my historical background. I am not the sort of person to correct them, but some do, and they can sometimes be rude and hurtful.

If you choose a well-known character, like Henry VIII, for example, it is important to learn and consider his character not just from an exterior viewpoint but from within. Imagine how he may have felt about his role and those around him. He would not have considered himself a bad fellow at all, and probably deemed those around him to be at fault.

For those on a smaller budget, a courtier further down the scale might be easier to represent. Their clothes, while splendid, would not be as extravagant as a noble or a royal member of court.

There are numerous books and websites you can visit. Pinterest is an invaluable source and YouTube is full of historical sewers sharing their talents and offering tips. It is very tempting to rush in and start sewing, but trust me, if you do the research first, you will avoid making costly mistakes.

As I have suggested previously, it is a good idea to make a complete mock-up before you cut into your expensive fabric. I used an old pair of curtains for my first attempt and the result was abysmal, but it didn't matter because it had cost me nothing. I later pulled the thing apart and reused the lining and boning in a later, more successful get-up.

The pattern on the curtaining doesn't matter for the practice piece but you will need the biggest pair you can find. The liner is useful for a shift and can also be used for lining the bodice and skirt. You can use old blankets for interlining at this stage and many people use heavy-duty plastic garden ties in place of boning. If your curtains aren't big enough, consider making your first garment for a child – a bit like a carpenter's apprentice would make a small cabinet, to save on material costs without scrimping on quality.

Give it your best shot, don't cut corners in the sewing or you will just end up with a dressing-up costume. Do it properly and your daughter/

granddaughter/niece/next door neighbour's child will be delighted, and you may even get them hooked and recruit them to your group. It is far easier to fit and sew a garment for someone else than it is to make one for yourself. Constant trying-on sessions can be difficult, but they are necessary, and you really need an assistant for the fitting when making your own outfit.

So, when you've determined that your sewing skills are up to it, chosen your character, checked group rules, and done your research, it is time to make your first (possibly child-sized) garments. Start from the skin out – although it is exciting to get to the fancy top layer, they will not sit correctly unless they are constructed over your base layer garments. It's a bit like making trifle, you'd never start with the whipped cream and strawberries, you'd wait for the jelly to set before you started.

When choosing your fabric (or old curtains), try to get something vaguely like damask silk, or velvet, but bear in mind velvet is very messy to work with and you must be aware of the 'nap'. If you are using curtains, when choosing them, always check the condition of the lining – if it is good, then it can be used for underpinnings and lining (which in your final garments should be silk or linen) but don't pass on a good pair just because the lining is stained, it might wash up or, if it is not suitable, you can always use a cotton sheet.

Gowns from the earlier period (1485–1509) are easier to make as the style requires less structure, but most people hanker for the iconic French gown, and I will be focusing on that style for the next few pages.

Constructing a Tudor coif

The coif is a simple garment for a novice sewer. You will need a half yard or so of linen, the grade will depend on the status of the historical character you are planning to re-enact. Coarser linen for the lower classes, with exceptionally fine linen for the upper classes. It is easier for a novice to work with the coarser fabric, as it is not so slippery.

Cut out your paper pattern, remembering to leave ¾ of an inch seam allowance. You will need two brim pieces, a circular piece, known as a 'bag', and two bands of the same length. (NB: you can cut the band in one piece, placing the long side on a fold and press well to reduce stitching time.)

Figure 50: Linen coif. (*Photograph: Judith Arnopp*)

First pin and sew the outer edge of the brim using back stitch. Trim seams and corners, notch curves. Turn and press.

Some people like to add a thin millinery wire to the brim at this stage, but I often omit this. Measure a piece of wire to fit along the outside edge of the brim. Bend it to the shape and slip it in between the two layers. Secure close to the edge with a row of small, neat running stitches.

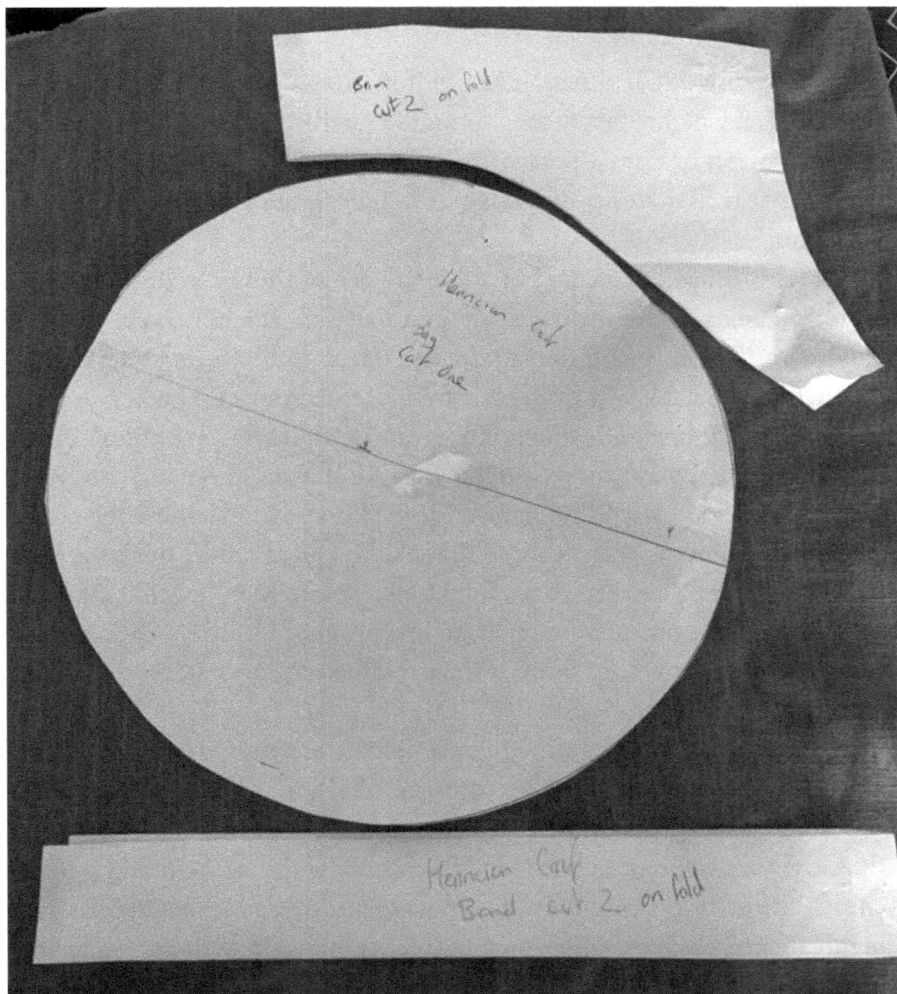

Figure 51: Tudor coif pattern pieces. (*Photograph: Judith Arnopp*)

Make a row of gathering stitches around the outer edge of the circular bag piece, and gently pull thread to required size to fit around the band. With right sides facing, stitch one edge of the band to the circle, adjusting the bag gathers to suit your taste. Press.

Stitch the other edge of the band to the brim. Press.

Turn and fold over edge of band to conceal all raw edges.

Some sewers close the band to form a circle, but I have found it useful to have it open to allow for adjustment at the nape of the neck.

Constructing a shift

Shifts were made of linen, coarser for the lower classes and fine handkerchief-weight for those of higher status, but for this practice garment, cotton or even a polycotton mix will suffice as long as you don't intend to wear it at Kentwell Hall or similar establishments/groups with strict rules.

Shifts are simple to make but there are a few things to bear in mind before you begin. When you cut out your pattern, whichever one you use, I advise you to leave the neckline edge uncut until the first trying-on session. Cut the back and front on a fold (see diagram) and when you try it on, make a slit just wide enough for your head, then using tailor's chalk or similar, mark where you would like it to sit on your chest and shoulders – you might need a friend to help you here. This will determine the cut of the *kirtle* neckline when you come to make it. Cut the shift neckline hole SMALLER than you require to allow for seams. Remember that cleavage and high, heaving bosoms are really an invention of Hollywood – very few Tudor portraits show bare flesh. If the neckline was low cut, then a partlet was usually worn for modesty.

Shifts are not a fitted garment, and neither are they flattering. I look really horrible in mine. They are constructed from a variety of geometric shapes and are supposed to hang loosely from the shoulders to mid-calf. Gores are inserted at the sides to provide width of hem and gussets beneath the arms provide room for movement. It is a loose and relatively unembellished garment which enabled it to stand up to regular laundering. The upper classes often had blackworked edge to the neck and cuffs, but the parts that would not be visible were left unadorned.

In the Tudor period, this garment was simple enough for most women to sew without the need for a tailor. Since they were frequently laundered, a woman would require several shifts or as many as she could afford. The most demanding thing I found when sewing a shift is the neatening of the many seams, so I cheat a little by machining a small hem all the way round the edge of the cut-out pattern pieces, then I whip stitch them together by hand.

Perfecting the gusset insert beneath the arms can be difficult and time consuming, but the method above removes the fiddly task of neatening the seams afterwards. Finally, I cut as small as possible a slit that my head will fit through before trying it on. My assistant (husband) then marks out the neckline. Then I either roll hem it, or if it has a lined bodice, I tuck in and press the two edges and whipstitch it closed, embellishing the edge with narrow cotton lace. NB: If blackwork trim is required, then this should be applied before constructing the garment, but remember to hem the pieces to prevent fraying as you work.

Constructing a farthingale

This is a modest garment but one that I find the most difficult to get right. The cone shape of the skirts depends on the correct shaping of this garment. Some people opt to buy one, but they can be shockingly expensive for a garment that is never seen. Some re-enactors choose to wear a Victorian crinoline petticoat, but although they are cheaper and easier to come by, the shape is not historically correct. As the diagram in the image below shows, the crinoline resembled a bell, it was round and wide while the farthingale was smaller, and cone shaped. On my first attempt, I used the Simplicity pattern, which came out completely the wrong shape because I didn't understand the importance of the measurements between the boning channels for the hoops. It was more an 'oops petticoat' than a 'hooped petticoat'.

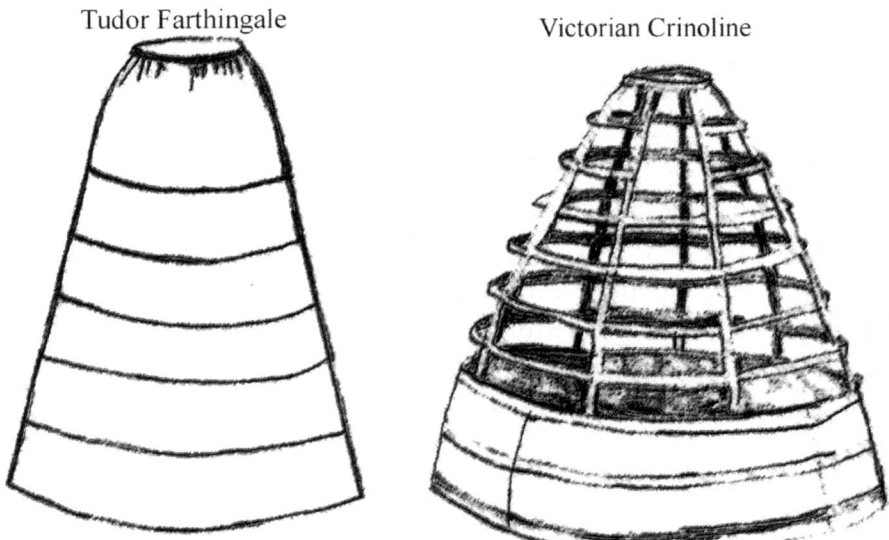

Tudor Farthingale

Victorian Crinoline

Figure 52: Diagram of crinoline and farthingale. (*Judith Arnopp*)

Patterns are available and there are instructions online to help you construct a farthingale. Pay particular attention to the measurement between each hoop and where it should lie on *your* body.

Royalty and nobility used silk for their farthingale but since yours is unlikely to be seen, you can use a cheaper fabric (but again, check with your group rules). Since the Tudors favoured red petticoats, some re-enactors make their farthingale up in red wool fabric, others use red linen or opt for simple unbleached calico or canvas. My advice is to make your first attempt from calico (or an old sheet) in case of mishap. Whatever fabric you decide to use, four yards of 54 inch wide should be enough – that is 3.6576 metres for the converted, I think.

Before you sew the pieces together, you need to mark the boning channels onto each piece and sew the hoop casings. This is not as difficult as it sounds, providing you get the markings correct and follow them exactly. You can use herringbone tape for this, although some re-enactors make rows of tucks to accommodate the hoops; since that method requires even more mathematics, I prefer the simpler technique of sewing on ready-made tape.

When you sew the side seams of the various farthingale pieces together, ensure you match the ends of the casing tape, but don't sew over them or you will not be able to insert your hoops. Take it slowly, take time to think. Try not to cry.

The waist can be a simple hem with a drawstring tie, or you can make a proper waistband with lacing holes. Now, it is time to insert your hoops, which is a snaggy task that is more frustrating and fiddlier than you might expect. Once all hoops are in place, you may find your finished farthingale is a very odd shape, but do not despair… not yet!

Try it on *before* you've sewed all the hoop casing ends closed. Get a friend to help you ensure the outline is as smooth a cone shape as you can manage – you may have to adjust several or all the hoops individually, either by cutting them or simply doubling the ends of the hoops over each other. I secured my practice piece together with gaffer tape but this, of course, is not the traditional way. It may still look an odd shape, but the final adjustments can be made once you've tried it on with kirtle and gown; sometimes the weight of the upper layers force the farthingale into compliance.

Before you decide to sew this garment, bear in mind that the style was not adopted by everyone. It arrived with Catherine of Aragon and wasn't immediately fashionable but grew popular later in the period. You could get away with not wearing one at all, but you will require a thick padded petticoat instead to achieve the required weight and volume.

Constructing a kirtle

The kirtle is an important layer. It forms the structure, supports the body, and helps provide that typical Tudor shape. It is lined and interlined, the skirt sometimes padded to ensure the lines of the farthingale hoops beneath cannot be seen through the fabric. The only parts of the kirtle that will show are the edge of the bodice at the neck, and the front panels

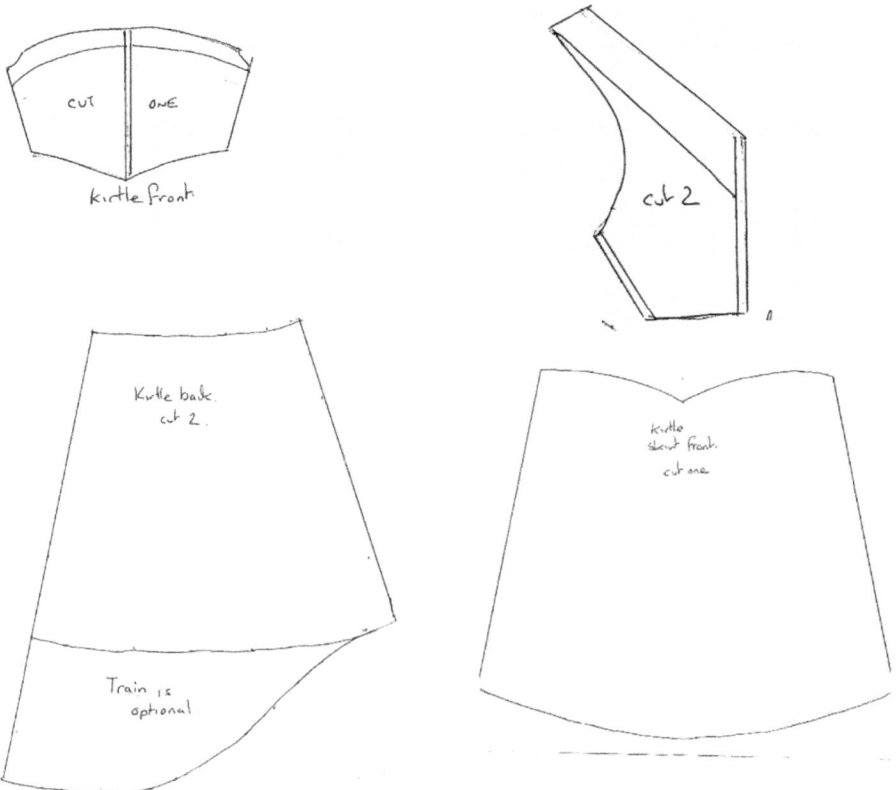

Figure 53: Diagram of kirtle pieces. (*Judith Arnopp*)

of the skirt. It is acceptable and very period authentic to cut these sections from quality fabric and use plainer materials for the areas that will not be on show.

NB: Remember to have enough kirtle fabric to make your matching inner sleeves, as traditionally kirtle and sleeves were made from the same cloth. The instructions below are for a garment using the Tudor Tailor pattern available online.

First, cut out your paper pattern. Note that the Tudor Tailor do not include a seam allowance in their patterns. You can either cut the paper pattern out three-eighths of an inch bigger or remember to include it when you cut the fabric. I tend to use the former method because I've a head like a sieve and cutting the fabric too small is nothing short of disaster.

Cut the bodice pieces in calico, top fabric and lining, *not forgetting the seam allowance* as indicated in the instructions. Then, for the interlining, cut them again from canvas (or buckram if you want it extra stiff), without a seam allowance. Tack the canvas pieces to the calico. Transfer boning channel marks (usually marked on the paper pattern by dotted lines) from the pattern to the calico – you can do this either with a contrasting shade of tacking stitches, or by using a washable fabric pen.

Sew along the boning channels, through both the canvas and the calico, and try to keep straight lines. *Do not sew the marked under-bust lines.* It can be tricky to get a good fit, but it is essential to do so at this stage – try it on over your shift and make sure the straps of the kirtle are comfortable and sit where you want them to lie over the square neck of your shift. If you don't make the necessary adjustments now, the whole outfit will not fit nicely. It is important not just for looks but for comfort, there is nothing worse than struggling with, or putting up with chafing from ill-fitting shoulder straps. (And I should know.) For the most recent kirtles I've sewn, I have made up the lining to fit perfectly and then unpicked it and cut out the top pieces using the lining as a pattern.

It is important to press your work between each step.

Once you are satisfied with the fit, sew side, back, and shoulder seams of bodice and press open the seam allowances. Repeat this step with the lining if you haven't made that first.

Insert bones into the sewn channels – you can buy these from online haberdashers, or many people use plastic garden ties from DIY hardware

Figure 54: Inside a kirtle bodice. (*Judith Arnopp*)

stores, but if you want to be historically accurate, you can purchase reed. Cut the bones so they do not go all the way to the bottom of the bodice, or you will encounter problems when it comes to attaching the skirt later on. Carefully sew the curved neckline.

Using a contrasting strip of fabric along the bodice edge, pin it to the neckline from the left shoulder strap to the right, covering all layers. If you prefer not to use contrasting fabric here, it is perfectly acceptable to use the same as your main kirtle. Turn under raw edges and sew all the way around to form a neat bound edge.

The skirt panels should now be sewn together with a ten-inch (26 cm) opening at the back (for a back-lacing gown). Sew the linings in the same way. Press open seam allowances.

There are two ways to tackle the skirt.

With right sides together, pin the lining to outer skirt, tacking top and bottom. Sew along the bottom edge. (I machine mine, to avoid some stitching time.)

Turn right side out and press neatly.

Refer to the pattern markings and form pleats along the top edge of skirt. For me, this is always the part where I want to give up. It may take

Figure 55: Back kirtle. (*Photograph: Judith Arnopp*)

quite a few attempts to get the pleats evenly spaced, but do not give up. The skirt will be heavy and difficult to manage if you do not have a wide enough work surface. I have found a wide pasting table is useful.

The other way of dealing with the skirt is to leave the hem unsewn, just tack the skirt and lining together and continue with the pleats, as in the previous paragraph.

The full width of the skirts needs to be pleated small enough to fit within the measurement of the bodice waist. Once happy with the pleats, pin, then tack and sew them in place.

Pin pleated skirt to the bottom of the bodice, right sides facing, and tack or sew. Take your time, this is a tricky bit. I usually tack mine first to make sure it is right. There is a lot of material to fit into a small bodice, which will seem impossible. I sometimes resort to sewing it to a narrow waistband and then stitch the waistband to the bodice lining; that isn't the correct way, and probably takes longer in the long run, but it preserves my sanity.

Before you are done, you will have sore fingers and eye strain but as you work, it helps to focus on the fabulous figure you will cut in your lovely new gown.

One you've securely sewn it on, give your fingers a rest and go and have a coffee, or a maybe a large gin.

If possible, put the bodice onto a form and assess the hang of the skirts before you sew the hem. It is advisable to leave it hanging overnight to allow the skirts to settle. The hem can be bound with velvet or a strip of the same fabric you've used for the main garment, but this isn't strictly necessary. Binding the hem can be tricky for a novice and the skirts can be hemmed in the usual way, but whichever method you choose, make sure you measure the length of the hem *over* the farthingale petticoat, or it will be too short!

Pin the lower edge of the bodice lining in place and slip stitch closed. Turn under the seam allowances at the back opening and, using your pattern markings, insert the eyelets. Metal eyelets are not historically accurate to our period, but many re-enactors use them. I used to hand sew over the metal eyelets, but it is tedious, and I have since discovered that handsewn lacing holes last just as long as metal ones. It is advisable to practise eyelet holes on a piece of scrap fabric but don't worry too much if they aren't very tidy, they will not be on show, functionality is more important than neatness.

Next comes the fun of sewing or pinning on your chosen ouches or jewels. Depending on your budget, you can either make these yourself with bits and pieces bought online, or you can buy the jewels ready-made. You will find filigree bases and faux pearls and gems on eBay and with careful use of the glue gun, you may be surprised at what you can achieve. Tudor-style jewellery can be pricey, but Etsy is a good place to start looking. I have a mixture of readymade and homemade bling but, as with the fabric, I find less is more… unless you can afford the real thing.

Usually, it is just the visible top neck edge of the kirtle that is decorated – further jewels will be required for the top gown, so I tend to keep the kirtle edging more modest, but that is a matter of choice. Alternatively, you can wait and sew all embellishments on when you have completed the top gown.

Constructing a Partlet

There are various partlet patterns to be found online but I can't comment on those because I made my own pattern. Mine is a working woman's garment that comes just below the bust and is meant to be worn over the top of a workaday kirtle. I made mine from linen, and like the kirtle, it is reversible, providing me with the option of a red or a black partlet. It is a very easy one-piece garment. I will give instructions for making the reversible option.

Cut the pieces from your required fabric and lining. You can use linen or lightweight wool for lower or middling-class costume, or silk or woven

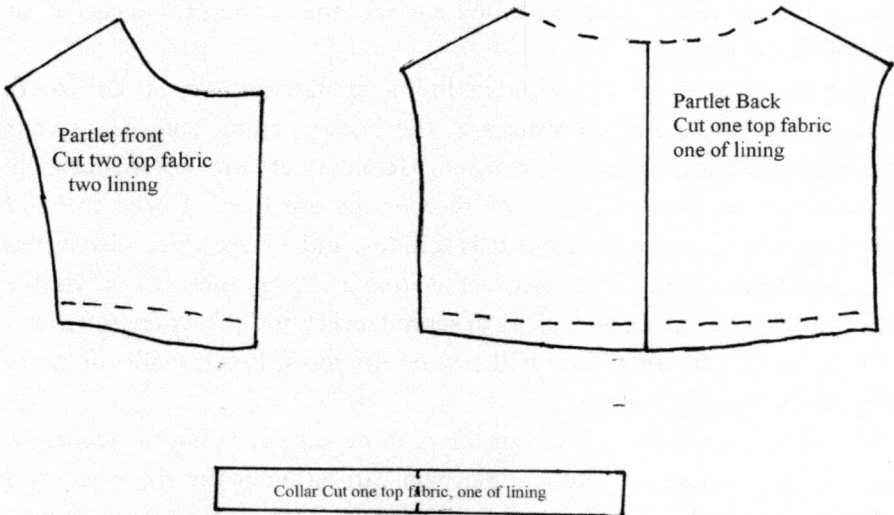

Partlet front
Cut two top fabric
two lining

Partlet Back
Cut one top fabric
one of lining

Collar Cut one top fabric, one of lining

Partlet: Please note seam allowance is not included

Figure 56: Diagram of reversible partlet pattern. (*Judith Arnopp*)

brocade fabric for upper class. With right sides together, sew the shoulder seams and press open. Lie the bodice pieces wrong sides together and press the seams of the two garments under before whip stitching together. I have not joined the underarm section but have added eyelets so it can be laced closed. It is also historically accurate to use pins to keep it closed. A lighter garment in this style was also worn beneath the kirtle and can be seen in many portraits. These were often sewn from a sheer fabric or very lightweight blackworked linen.

Constructing the top gown

The top gown provides the real wow factor and should be made from the very best fabric you can acquire. Tudors would have chosen silk or silk taffeta, brocade or velvet with fur trimming to the sleeves. Since I don't have their budget, I usually opt for a large pair of damask jacquard curtains. You can make a gown in a size 20–22 from a 90 x 90 pair. The Simplicity pattern doesn't look too bad from a distance, but it is far from an authentic representation so, as before, I will use the Tudor Tailor pattern. The instructions that come with these patterns can sound complicated for a novice sewer, but an online search will provide various blogs with illustrated details of how to put it together. YouTube videos are also invaluable to clarify the task but also make it look easy. Just remember, there is no hurry. Take it slowly.

You will need to cut the pattern pieces from top fabric, lining, and interlining. A silk or faux silk lining is advisable on the skirt, particularly if you are using a light silk, as the front opening sometimes blows back, revealing the inner, and I think it is important that the inside fabric is pretty. It is not necessary to line the whole skirt, just the front sections.

Depending on your size, the gown will require up to nine metres of fabric, it may be more if you require a train or the wider style of skirts and sleeves. You will also need roughly the same amount of calico for interlining and silk or taffeta (or the faux equivalent) for lining. A further two to three metres will be required for turn-back sleeves in faux fur or silk. I have used linen for the bodice lining as it is more comfortable and cooler to wear than synthetic silk, but I haven't found it very much cheaper.

As with the kirtle, it is wise to cut out the bodice pieces in calico first and stitch them together to get a good fit. Pay attention to the fit of the shoulder, which can be complex with the wide Tudor neckline. Try it on over your completed kirtle and shift to ensure the neckline sits where you want it to over the kirtle. When you are happy with the fit and the way the three layers work together, it is safe to continue to cut into your expensive material. This is always a nerve-racking experience.

Although silky fabrics are lovely and the patterns are fun, they make life more difficult for the novice sewer. Silk is slippery and can be awkward for a novice to work with. I would also advise you to avoid stretch velvet as you would the plague or the sweating sickness; it is not only historically inaccurate but beastly to work with. Pattern matching is not too difficult, but it is advisable to make your first gown from plain fabric to avoid this and the potholes that can open up by using silky patterned fabrics. There will be plenty of time to make fancier gowns once you have mastered how to put them together.

Starting with the bodice back, place the top fabric and interlining pieces wrong sides together and tack.

Repeat for all back and side pieces.

The front pieces will be covered with a placard so can be cut from cheaper fabric of similar hue. Cut the front pieces from lining, interlining, and top fabric. Baste the interlining and top fabric together. Place the top fabric and lining right sides together and stitch along the centre front line.

Mark and sew the boning channels (see dotted lines on your pattern), then fold the upper edges in and stitch neatly. Insert bones into the channels and mark your eyelet holes as indicated on the pattern. These should be staggered to allow for spiral lacing, which is not only historically accurate but makes it easier when it comes to getting dressed and undressed.

Join the front bodice side edge to the back bodice.

Fold in the neck edges and stitch neatly. Try the bodice on and pray that it still fits correctly.

Now it is time to construct the sleeves, which should be cut from top fabric, lining, and interlining. Ensure you cut them with the right sides of the top fabric together or you will end up with two right sleeves. Tack the top fabric and interlining together, fold so the right sides are facing and sew. Turn the sleeves the right way out, fold back the hem and stitch it in place. Press.

Pin the sleeve into the armhole and sew. NB: At this stage, before I attach the sleeve, I insert the lining and clean finish the arm hole of the bodice and the shoulder seam of the sleeve. That way, I can whip stitch the two together. It sounds an odd way of tackling the job, but I find that if I stitch carefully, I get a cleaner neater and less bulky finish that way.

If you prefer to do it the traditional way, trim and notch the curved seams to ensure the join lies smoothly.

Repeat the same steps for the lining, starting with the back and side pieces of the bodice, and insert the sleeves before fitting the lining into the bodice and slip stitching together.

Remember the battle you had attaching the kirtle skirt to the bodice? Now you must do the same with the gown – there may be even more bulk to tackle this time. As before, the skirt pieces should be cut from top fabric, interlining (if you are using it), and lining. Baste the interlining and top fabric together along the top and bottom edge. Join the skirt side seams and then do the same with the lining. Put the lining and fabric right sides together and pin and sew along the bottom hem, turn, and press. (I use the machine for these long seams.) If you wish to bind the hem and the front edges of the gown, there are instructions for this to be found online.

Now it is time to tackle the pleats. You can choose whether to use box or cartridge pleats, or a combination of knife and cartridge pleats, but box pleats are more accurate for an early-style gown. It is important to practice pleating on some scrap fabric before you sew them into place. Some people pad the pleats to add volume, but I have adequate volume if I wear a bum roll, which does away with the need for further stuffing.

You then whip stitch the pleats together, but I often skip this step and just tack and stitch them to the bodice, repeating the steps used in the construction of the kirtle. If you have already sewed the lining and outer hem together, care must be taken at this stage to check the length of the skirt over the farthingale and kirtle and ensure that any required adjustments to the length are made at the waist of the skirt.

After the battle you've fought sewing the gown, the placard is a piece of cake!

Cut the pieces from interlining, lining, and top fabric. If the material you are using is quite light, then use more interlining – buckram and one layer of linen or calico is ideal.

Run a boning channel down the centre front of the placard by placing the interlining together and sewing a narrow double seam, ensuring you leave enough space to accommodate your choice of bone. You can also work many channels up and down the placard to stiffen the fabric, but you will not need to bone those channels.

Place the buckram and interlining on the wrong side of the top fabric, fold the top edge under and baste to the interlining. Then apply the lining by placing it wrong side down, turning the edge in, and neatly tacking and stitching in place. It might help to press a small hem along all edges of the lining before you begin this step.

A Tudor lady's placard would have been secured to her gown with pins but that can be a tricky method for the busy re-enactor. You can buy authentic brass pins from Etsy, but they can be difficult to keep in place and some re-enactors stitch one side of the placard and just pin the other, some use hooks and eyes. I've even seen some people resort to Velcro but… please, no.

Fore sleeves

Fore sleeves (sometimes referred to as inner sleeves) are purely for show and the fabric usually matches the skirt or forepart of the kirtle. They cover the arm from wrist to just above the elbow and are fastened to the inside of the gown sleeve with points or linen ties. Explaining the method of sewing this stage of the costume makes it sound far more complex than it actually is. I suggest you examine some portraits of the sleeves you'd like to wear to give you a clearer idea of your final goal.

To make the sleeves, you will require one metre of top fabric and lining, and a small amount of white linen or silk for the puffed slashes. For a simpler sleeve, you can omit the puffs and just have the white linen along the sleeve opening, which gives the impression of linen beneath. Fore sleeves are also decorated with ouches or individual pearls. In fact, you can make them as fancy as you please.

Cut out your sleeve pieces in top fabric and lining; if you are using exceptionally light fabric, you may like to add an interlining. There are two ways you can construct your sleeves. Usually, by this stage, I am feeling pretty sewed out, so there is a quicker method as well as a longer but prettier, and possibly more accurate, option.

Option one: Place the top fabric and lining right sides together, pin, and sew. Turn the right way out, turn in the hem of the remaining open seam

Figure 57: Sleeve. (*Photograph: Judith Arnopp*)

and slip stitch closed. Press. The sleeve is then folded, the curved edge is positioned beneath your arm and fastened along the edge with ouches. Before you do this, however, you need to add the white linen puffed pane. The easiest way is to sew a linen tube, like a sausage, and lightly stuff it. Work out where you wish your fastenings to be on the actual sleeve and oversew the stuffed linen tube at these measurements. You will now have what resembles a string of white linen sausages. This then needs to be stitched along the bottom open edge of your sleeve, positioned half in and half out of the two open seams so that the white linen peeks from between the fastenings. Play with the puffs until you are happy with the appearance and stitch securely in place. Ouches are then placed at each closure along the sleeve in between each sausage.

Option two: You will need to cut the sleeve pieces as before from top fabric, lining, and interlining of calico or similar. Then cut again from canvas but omitting the seam allowance. Tack the canvas to the calico interlining and the calico to the reverse side of the top fabric.

Using the pattern, take a pencil or fabric pen and mark the cut-out sections to the wrong side of the fabric and tack. To bind the holes, cut rectangles of silk lining fabric large enough to cover the cut-out sections, and sew around on the pencil marks. Once stitched, you can carefully snip out the fabric in the centres with a small pair of scissors, leaving a narrow seam allowance. Turn lining fabric through the hole to the wrong side. Press edges neatly and tack in place. You should now have a neat contrasting edge around your cut-out holes.

Cut further rectangles of white silk or linen (or something similar). The idea is that it should look as if your fine undergarments are peeping through the holes in your sleeve. Sew running stitches along the longer sides and gather slightly before pinning the rectangle to the back of the hole, arranging them to your satisfaction as you go. Ensuring you penetrate all layers using small even stitches, sew all around the edge of each hole.

With the wrong sides together, pin or tack the lining and sleeve together. Then take a roughly 4 cm strip of contrasting fabric – if your gown is plain and your sleeves patterned, you might like to use a plain strip, or vice versa if your gown is patterned.

You now need to press under both edges of the strip to form a binding. Then pin and sew the binding right sides facing all around the outer sleeve edge, catching all layers. When you reach the end, turn the remaining edge out, pin, and slip stitch in place.

Finally, as in option one, you need to construct the 'pulling out' from fine linen, silk, or similar fabric. To ensure you cut the right length, measure the outer edge of your sleeve (the open side) and add a seam allowance. Create the tube of sausages as before and pin the pullings-out into place on the sleeve. The gathered point should be hidden by the place you will add fastenings, the puffed sections will peek becomingly from your sleeve. Sew into place and add your jewelled fastenings.

If your chemise/shift/smock does not have a fancy cuff, do not despair. It was commonplace for cuffs to be worn as a separate garment to allow for easy laundering. They were often, but not always, embroidered. They can be fastened with ties at the wrist or (since it won't be seen) you can use hooks and eyes or even press studs. The first I made were plain, but I have since experimented with a cheat's method of blackwork. I discovered a lady on Etsy selling a black work design printed onto a strip of linen-like fabric. It is just the right size to work into a cuff or collar and from a distance it looks convincing. I embroidered over mine with black silk, which is far easier than all the thread counting that proper black work requires and it makes it appear that I am a far better needlewoman than I really am. If you are really posh you can include seed pearls in your design.

Constructing a French hood

I will do my best to explain how to make both styles of French hood that we discussed earlier in the book, but before you decide which to make, you might want to bear in mind that the new idea I detailed in Chapter Four is not only more comfortable to wear but far simpler to make. However, first I will address the hood that has been worn traditionally by re-enactors and Hollywood.

This hood is not a simple make, and it is quite likely your first attempt may not be wholly successful but, as with most things, trial and error is part of the process. My advice is to use cheaper materials for your first attempt.

The base of the hood is constructed from buckram and millinery wire, and sewing it can be quite tough on the fingers. There are various patterns available and there were several different shapes and styles, so study the patterns carefully and decide which best suits your needs.

Your pattern will be in three parts: the head piece, the crescent, and the veil.

Take your pattern and cut it from buckram (a stiff canvas available from the Tudor Tailor online). It can be stiff to cut out. Cut the same shape from something soft, like flannel or scraps of woollen material. This will prevent the stiff buckram from rubbing your ears and making them sore. Whip stitch these two pieces over the buckram, keeping the edges as tidy as possible.

Using a heavy-duty thread, stitch millinery wire around the outer edge of your base and the crescent. You may need to resort to pliers to ensure you follow the shape precisely. It is important to somehow soften the ends of the wire – I usually resort to bending it back on itself, wrapping it in a scrap of soft lining, and securing it with a blob of glue from my glue gun. This is cheating, of course, but after all, it will not be seen.

Your work may be an odd shape at this stage, but do not discard it, it may yet come right.

Now it is time to cut your pattern from top fabric and whatever material you plan to use as lining. This should be cut half an inch wider than the buckram base you have sewn. (Please note: if you want to be authentic as possible, French hoods were almost always red and black and did not match the gown, there is no explanation for this that I could find.)

I often see recommendations for silk or satin inner for French hoods, but if you have fine silky hair, it is difficult to make them stay on. I usually opt for black linen, which clings to the hair (or coif) better. The outer fabric that will be on show can be silk or velvet. Also, to ensure it stays in place, try to style your hair in braids, as discussed in Chapter Ten.

Place the cut-out pieces right sides together and sew along the shaped edge of the base and the upper edge of the crescent. Trim the seam allowances and notch the curves before turning the right side out. Press. Then, ease your covered buckram pieces inside, position them neatly and, using small stitches, whip the open edges of the top fabric closed. It may take some easing and wriggling to get this right, but endeavour to get it as taut as you can. Remember to press between each stage of the construction.

Position the crescent centrally on the base, leaving a small lip of the base showing at the front and stitch firmly. A curved needle is useful at his stage. Try to keep your stitches as small as you can but don't worry if they are a little uneven, for they can be hidden with pearls when we reach the fun 'billament' stage.

The veil is almost always made from velvet. I have made them for customers who requested a silky tulle fabric, and this does look nice but is not authentic. If you want to go with the sheer veil, it is best to check with your group first. Cut out the pattern piece and hem the edges. It may not tell you to do this on the pattern instructions that you have, but I find it is easier to hem it at this stage.

The veil attaches to the back of the *base*, NOT the crescent. Find the centre point on the base of your buckram head piece and pin the veil evenly before stitching. If you do not check that it is central, with the top of the curve positioned correctly, your veil will not hang straight.

As I mentioned before, even with a coif, I have had trouble keeping this style of hood in place during an active re-enactment. I know that some re-enactors have no problems, but I am not particularly lady-like and am forever banging the stiff crescent and dislodging it. When I first began wearing one, I resorted to a lot of hat pins, but when I tried it with an authentic hairstyle, it was much easier to secure. If you have long hair and can use your braids, wrapped about your head, to secure it, you should have no problems.

Now is time to add the billaments to your hood. Before you start smothering it with large blingy jewels, examine the portraits and copy one you fancy as closely as you can. I find pearls or braid positioned along the (usually) untidy sewn join between the base and crescent hides a multitude of sins. I thread mine onto very thin wire and neatly stitch in place. I do the same along the top edge of the crescent.

The no-buckram French hood

The 'no-buckram' hood is much simpler to construct than the usual style, and I strongly suggest you watch the YouTube videos I mentioned previously before you begin so you understand the relevance and reasons behind this innovative change.

This style is in three parts. It comprises linen coif, red silk cap, and black velvet hood but you can cheat and make it using just two if you wish by omitting the coif, and instead lining the red silk cap with linen and adding the gold pleated trim to the front edge of the red cap.

You may already have a coif, so first you need to make a red silk cap. This is a simple construction, lined with white linen and edged with pleated organza frill. It is basically a rectangle of top fabric, another of white linen. There is no seam at the top, so the long side wraps over the head and around the face with the short side ending at your jawline.

With right sides facing, sew the lining and red silk together along one short side and both long sides. Trim seam allowance and corners. Turn the right side out and press neatly. (NB: You can either apply the organza trim now on the outside, or you can sandwich it between one of the long edges of the silk and linen before stitching together.)

Fold the piece in half and neatly slip stitch the short seam, you may find you need to stitch both silk and linen inside and out to make it neat.

At the back of the neck, insert a channel for the ties. You can do this by sewing a seam parallel to the bottom hem and making eyelet holes in the top fabric, or by adding a hemmed strip of fabric to the lining. Thread narrow ties through the channel. These ties will be wrapped up the back of your head around your braided hair (provided your hair is long enough to braid). Again, I recommend the Tudor Tailor's short video showing you how to style your hair for a secure fit.

The hood part is constructed from black velvet with a white linen lining for the head piece only. I have found it better to reinforce the headpiece with an additional interlining to help it keep its shape. A thick linen or even hessian will suffice.

The first step is to cut the T-shape and trim away the two lower corners of the head piece as indicated in the diagram (see Figure 58). Baste the inner lining to the outer edges of the headpiece lining, place the lining

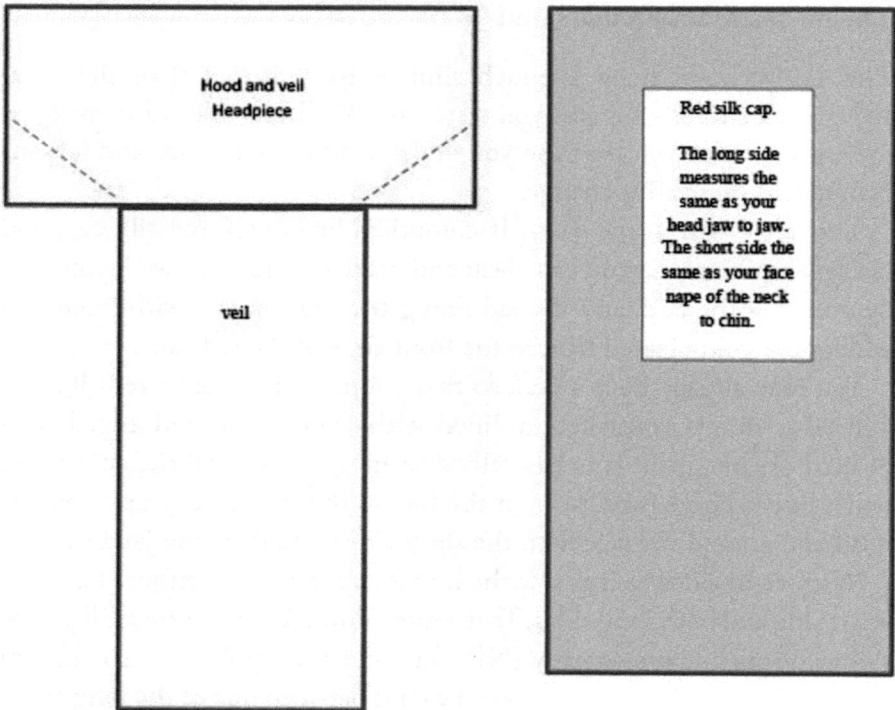

Hood and veil
Headpiece

veil

Red silk cap.

The long side measures the same as your head jaw to jaw. The short side the same as your face nape of the neck to chin.

Guide for the construction of the three layered French Hood (not to scale)

Figure 58: Diagram of French hood pattern. (*Judith Arnopp*)

and top fabric wrong sides together, and slip stitch. Hem the three sides of the veil (alternatively, you could do this before you stitch the first step). You will now have a roughly T-shaped piece, of which the horizontal piece is lined with linen, the lower veil piece remains unlined, although you can line it if you require a stiffer veil. The veil should be a tube, so neatly place the two long edges together and slip stitch them closed.

You can now try it on. As with most garments, you may need to make some adjustments to ensure a good fit. If your gown is of an early style, the hood was left quite plain; later in the period, pastes and billaments were added.

Constructing a gabled hood

Making a gabled hood is far more complex than the French hood. There are different styles, the frontlets can be jaw length or a couple of inches below the chin. The materials you will need are as follows:

- A strip of paste buckram, a slightly larger strip of soft padding to wrap around the buckram and to pad out the lappets.
- White linen (or similar) for under cap and lining.
- Damask brocade or similar for lappets.
- Black cotton velvet or silk for back box and veil.
- A narrow strip of striped silk (or similar).
- Millinery wire.

If you are on a budget, you can get away with faux silk and cotton but, as I have said before, try not to choose anything too shiny. I know some re-enactors use cardboard to form the gable shape and cover that in fabric, but if you do, remember not to wear it in the rain.

As always, make a trial hood out of cheap materials before you start work on the final one. It is a good idea to examine contemporary portraits to help you decide on the shape and use a strip of cardboard about four inches (10 cm) wide and bend it into a gable shape and try out what height, width, or overall shape suits you best.

I usually begin by forming the gabled part of the construction and fitting the rest to it once I am happy with the size and shape.

NB: When I attempted my first prototype, instead of making the box part from buckram, I cheated and made mine from a cardboard box that once contained dishwasher tablets. It was the perfect size but since box sizes and heads differ, it is advisable to check that the box sits neatly on the back of your head.

Cut the under cap and box pieces from buckram, build the box, whip stitching or gluing the edges together. Run millinery wire around the edges of the gabled under cap. Stitch in place. NB: Please read to the end of this section before beginning work on this step. You can either cover the box pieces in velvet now before you assemble or later.

Cut the pattern again in soft interlining and cover the buckram and wire, then baste it in place. You may need to clip the inner seams around the curves to make the interlining lie flat.

Cut top fabric pieces, not forgetting to leave a seam allowance and attach to the wired base, overlapping the edges.

Cut lining fabric for under cap, pin in place, turning seam allowance under before sewing.

Bend into shape and pin the back into place, securing with small, neat stitches. Then bend again into a pleasing shape, tweaking the lower chin area to suit.

Next cut strips of striped silk (or similar). I found it difficult to source striped silk, so I used a fabric pen and a ruler and faked my own by drawing thick black stripes by hand. It is advisable to add padded rolls of silk or linen behind to help keep the hood in place on your head.

Cover your buckram (or cardboard) box in black velvet or silk, and line with linen. I find it easier to do this before constructing the box at the start and neatly stitch the covered pieces together.

Cut out veil strips from velvet and interlining, pin together, and sew down the two long and one short edge. Trim seam allowance, turn right sides out, and press. Turn in raw edges and slip stitch closed. You should now have two long strips or tails of velvet which can now be attached to the bottom of the velvet box.

Stitch the box to the back of the under cap, using small, neat stitches. If your stitches are not as neat as they should be, you can cover with braid later on.

Cut lapets in silk or similar, leaving a seam allowance, and cut the interlining with no seam allowance.

Figure 59: Detail from *Nonsuch Palace* by Joris Hoefnagel showing women wearing a bongrace. (*Wikimedia Commons*)

Baste interlining and top fabric together. Fold and stitch down one side before turning right side out. Turn in raw edges on open seam and stitch closed. Pin and stitch to the hood, folding the long tails back up and over the top. Contemporary portraits show the lapets were arranged in a variety of ways, sometimes left long, sometime pinned to the top of the hood, sometimes one was pinned and the other left down. See Holbein's sketches in Figures 16 and 22 for illustrations of Tudor gable hoods.

The bongrace (see the lady on the right in Figure 59) was a plainer, unembellished style of hood worn with the veil flipped up and over the back of the head, forming a peak. It was usually made from linen or lightweight wool or, for upper classes, velvet or silk. I have one I made to wear with my English-style gown. I wear a linen coif beneath it that frames my face, but that is for vanity reasons. In the image, the lady on the left is wearing a later style of cap beneath. The bongrace is a simple form of headwear to make. The Tudor Tailor has a pattern for one in the book, although to get it to flip over my head enough, I had to cut the hood part of the pattern longer than the one provided.

Figure 60: Disastrous first attempt at a Tudor gown. (*Photograph: Judith Arnopp*)

I am not an expert sewer, I have not been trained. As with most of my crafting skills, I have learned by trial and error. My very first attempt at a Tudor gown was bad, there is no denying that, so I am extremely glad I made it from cheap curtains. I cringe at showing you the photograph (Figure 60), but I want to reassure you that if your first attempt is similarly bad, your next will be better.

Figure 61: Fitting for a king. (*Photograph: Judith Arnopp*)

There are far, far better sewers than me out there, but I was unwilling to be left out because I couldn't justify the price of a new custom-made gown. Because it is so much cheaper to sew your own, learning to sew acceptable Tudor gowns has enabled me to make myself a whole wardrobe. I can now take part in re-enactments from different eras and my Tudor wardrobe is far more replete than my modern closet. I have not only made things from various eras but also for different social groups. I've made clothes for children, servants, ladies, and gentleman. While I play Elizabeth Stafford, my husband plays her spouse, the Duke of Norfolk, and I have even had a go at an outfit for King Henry VIII. There is nothing more nerve-racking than the king turning up for a fitting. I always worry that if he hates it, I will end up in the Tower and maybe even lose my head!

Like every other form of dressmaking, historical sewing should be fun. Just be aware that you will make mistakes, you will struggle with fit, with style, and in the early stages, you may wish you'd never started. But that will pass and then you'll be ready to join your group for your first re-enactment day and you'll be hooked.

There will be cold wet days and boiling hot days, you will have sore fingers, an empty bank balance, and aching feet, but it will be worth it. There is nothing like the smell of a campfire, the clash of swords, the salute from a passing soldier, a curtsey from a serving maid. This book will hopefully provide the first step on your re-enactment journey. Whatever your aim, be it for re-enactment or fancy dress, the sense of achievement when you've created your first, wobbly seamed, badly fitting Tudor gown is second to none. You will look in the mirror and either give it up as a bad job and chalk it up to experience, or you will pick up the challenge and go on to make a better one.

Notes

Introduction
1. E. Lynn, *Tudor Fashion* (2017), p. 66.
2. *Black's Law Dictionary* (6th ed.) (1999), p. 1436.
3. R. Goodman, *How to Be a Tudor: A Dawn-to-Dusk Guide to Tudor Life* (2015).
4. M. St Clare Burn, *The Lisle Letters*, 4 (letter 896) (1981), p. 167–168.
5. Lynn, p. 15.
6. Lynn, p.12.
7. A. Tinniswood, *Behind the Throne: A Domestic History of the Royal Household* (2018).

Chapter Two
1. S. Bendall, *Shaping Femininity: Foundation Garments, the Body and Women in Early Modern England* (2022), p. 27.

Chapter Four
1. Edward Hall, *Hall's chronicle containing the history of England during the reign of Henry the Fourth and the succeeding monarchs to the end of the reign of Henry the Eighth in which are particularly described the manners and customs of those periods* (2016).

Chapter Five
1. M. Hayward, *Dress at the Court of Henry VIII* (2007), p. 302.
2. Hayward, p. 302.
3. NB: It is advisable never to use any TV drama as inspiration for a Tudor gown if you are hoping for authenticity.
4. G. Chaucer, *The Canterbury Tales* (1971), p. 105.
5. Goodwin, *Blackwork Embroidery: Techniques and Projects* (2020), p. 10.
6. Hayward, p. 179.
7. N. Sander, *The Rise and Growth of the Anglican Schism* (1573), p. 25.
8. *Letters and Papers Foreign and Domestic. Calendar of Henry VIII* (1896) xv, p. 22.
9. *Letters and Papers* xv, p. 22.
10. J. Dillon, *Performance and Spectacle in Hall's Chronicle* (2002), p. 163.
11. *Letters and Papers* xv, p. 908.
12. *Letters and Papers* xv, pp. 565, 686.
13. *Letters and Papers* xvii, p. 63.
14. 'Henry VIII: August 1536, 1–5', in *Letters and Papers, Foreign and Domestic, Henry VIII, Volume 11, July–December 1536*, ed. James Gairdner (London, 1888), pp. 90–103. British History Online, www.british-history.ac.uk/letters-papers-hen8/vol11/pp90-103 (accessed 29 January 2022).

15. Lynn, p. 96.
16. D'Ewes, *The Journals o all the Parliament during the Reign of Queen Elizabeth both of the House of Lords and House of Commons collected by Sir Simonds D'Ewes of Stow Hall in the County of Suffolk* (1682), p. 339.

Chapter Six
1. P. Stubbes & J. P. Collier, *The Anatomie of Abuses* (2018).

Chapter Seven
1. Stubbes & Collier.
2. J. L. Carlson, *A Short History of the Monmouth Cap.* http://web.archive.org/web/20210126074907/http://www.personal.utulsa.edu/~Marc-Carlson/jennifer/Monmouth.htm (accessed 10 March 2021).

Chapter Eight
1. www.british-history.ac.uk/letters-papers-hen8/vol3/cx-clxvi
2. W. Hooper. 'The Tudor Sumptuary Laws' (1915), p. 445.
3. www.british-history.ac.uk/lords-jrnl/vol11/pp422-423#p9
4. A. Weir, *Henry VIII: King and Court* (2001), p. 188.
5. Weir, p. 190.
6. G. Cavendish, *The Life of Cardinal Wolsey* (2017), p. 125.

Chapter Nine
1. Erasmus, *Praise of Folly* (1989), p. 119.
2. C. Herbermann, ed. 'Rule of St. Benedict.' *Catholic Encyclopedia* (1913).
3. W. Map, *De Nugis Curialium: Courtiers' Trifles* (1983), p. 103.
4. D. Robinson, *The Cistercian Abbeys of Britain: Far from the Concourse of Men* (1999), p. 29.

Chapter Ten
1. J. Huggett & N. Mikhaila, *The Tudor Child* (2013), p. 7.
2. J. Sharp, *The Midwives Book or the Whole Art of Midwifry Discovered* (1671), p. 272.
3. W. Cadogan, 1711–1797, 2012, *An essay upon nursing: and the management of children, from their birth to three years of age. By a physician. In a letter to one of the governors of the Foundling Hospital. Published by order of the General Committee...*, Oxford Text Archive, http://hdl.handle.net/20.500.12024/K000335.000.
4. R. E. Pritchard, *Sex, Love and Marriage in the Elizabethan Age* (2021).
5. N. Mikhaila & J. Malcolm-Davies, *The Tudor Tailor*, p. 20.
6. 'Venice: May 1527', *Calendar of State Papers Relating to English Affairs in the Archives of Venice*, Volume 4: 1527–1533 (1871), pp. 56–66.

Bibliography

Bendall, Sarah, A., *Shaping Femininity: Foundation Garments, the Body and Women in Early Modern England* (Bloomsbury Publishing, London, 2022)

Black's Law Dictionary (6th edn.) (West Group, New York, 1999)

Buck, Anne, *Clothes and the Child* (Ruth Bean Publishers, Bedford, 1996)

Cavendish, George, *The Life of Cardinal Wolsey*, ed. Samuel Weller Singer (Createspace, London, 2017)

Chaucer, Geoffrey, *The Canterbury Tales*, ed. John Halverson (Bobbs-Merrill, New York, 1971)

D'Ewes, Simon, *The Journals o all the Parliament during the Reign of Queen Elizabeth both of the House of Lords and House of Commons collected by Sir Simonds D'Ewes of Stow Hall in the County of Suffolk* (Irish University Press, Shannon, 1682)

Dillon, Janette, *Performance and Spectacle in Hall's Chronicle* (The Society for Theatre Research, London, 2002)

Erasmus, D., *The Praise of Folly and Other Writings: A New Translation with Critical Commentary* (W. W. Norton & Company, New York, 1989)

Goodman, Ruth, *How to Be a Tudor* (Penguin, New York, 2015)

Goodwin, Jen, *Blackwork Embroidery: Techniques and Projects* (Crowood Press, Marlborough, 2020)

Hall, Edward, *Hall's chronicle containing the history of England during the reign of Henry the Fourth and the succeeding monarchs to the end of the reign of Henry the Eighth in which are particularly described the manners and customs of those periods* (2016)

Hayward, Maria, *Dress at the Court of Henry VIII* (Routledge, London, 2007)

Hooper, Wilfred, 'The Tudor sumptuary laws.' *English Historical Review* 30 (1915), 433–449.

Huggett, Jane and Mikhaila, Ninya, *The Tudor Child: Clothing and Culture 1485–1625* (Fat Goose Press, Surrey, 2013)

Johnson, Caroline, *The King's Servants* (The Tudor Tailor, Nottingham, 2009)

Johnson, Caroline, *The Queen's Servants* (The Tudor Tailor, Nottingham, 2011)

Letters and Papers Foreign and Domestic. Calendar of Henry VIII. Great Britain. Public Record Office, Henry VIII (King of England), 1896

Lynn, Eleri, *Tudor Fashion* (Yale University Press, New Haven, 2017)

Map, Walter, *De Nugis Curialium: Courtiers' Trifles*, ed. and tr. M. R. James, rev. C. N. L. Brooke and R. A. B. Mynors (Oxford University Press, Oxford, 1983)

Marston, John, *The Works of John Marston, Volume 2*, ed. Arthur Henry Bullen (Nimmo, Edinburgh, 1887)

Mikhaila, Ninya and Malcolm-Davies, Jane, *The Tudor Tailor: Reconstructing Sixteenth Century Dress* (Batsford, London, 2006)

Norris, Herbert, *Tudor Costume and Fashion* (Dover, New York, 1997)

Pritchard, R. E., *Sex, Love and Marriage in the Elizabethan Age* (Pen and Sword, Barnsley, 2021)

Rye, William Brenchley, *England as Seen by Foreigners, in the Days of Elizabeth and James the First* (John Russell Smith, London, 1865)

Sander, Nicholas, *The Rise and Growth of the Anglican Schism* (London, 1573)

Southworth, John, *Fools and Jesters at the English Court* (The History Press, London, 2003)

Stubbes, Phillip and Collier, John P., *The Anatomie of Abuses* (London, 2018)

Tinniswood, Adrian, *Behind the Throne: A Domestic History of the Royal Household* (Jonathan Cape, London, 2018)

Weir, Alison, *Henry VIII: King and Court* (Vintage, London, 2001)

Index